SO YOU HAVE A WEBSITE...
NOW WHAT?

WAYNE MULLINS

Copyright © 2012 by Wayne Mullins
All rights reserved.

ISBN-10: 147761902X
EAN-13: 9781477619025

To…
Heather my honey,
Truett my warrior,
Jett my joy,
and Hudson my ham.

Contents

Introduction	vii
1. Turning a Hobby into a Profitable Business	1
2. The Natural Progression	5
3. The Texas Two-Step	13
4. Continue the Conversation	11
5. But What If I'm All Alone?	17
6. Get Traffic Now	21
7. Long-Term Traffic Strategies	27
8. Search Engine Optimization (SEO)	43
9. Pay-Per-Click Advertising	65
10. Social Media	81
11. Thirteen Questions	95
12. You and I Are the Same	99
Thanks	101
Free ($497.00) Online Course	105

Introduction

You invested your time, tons of energy and effort, and all that money building a website for a specific purpose. Maybe you wanted to achieve a business or a personal goal. Maybe you wanted to get a step closer to your dreams. Or maybe you hoped it would become a tool to help you change the world.

But if your website is like most, it has done nothing more than bring you frustration. Websites are often built under false pretenses. People deceive themselves into believing that having a website will be their "magic bullet"—the solution to all their problems.

The Grand Illusion

I was new to business. My hopes were high, and even higher were my dreams for my life and my business. I had just stepped out on my own and started a lawn and landscape company.

I didn't know much about business; but the one thing I did know was this: once I had a website developed, my business would immediately be catapulted toward success. After all, it was the early 2000s, and even though we had just come off the "tech bubble burst," the media still ran rampant with overnight Internet success stories.

And I was determined to become one of them.

With hopes and visions of success in hand, I picked up the phone to call a local website designer. I'll admit I was a bit fearful, even before I dialed him. Would he crush all my hopes and dreams of overnight success?

So I carefully, cautiously bared my soul to him, detailing how this website would not only help me dominate my local market, but quickly allow me to dominate the entire state. To my amazement, he didn't crush my hopes and dreams. Nope, he actually added fuel to the fire.

He said that, with his help, I would soon be able to realize my hopes and dreams. So I put all those hopes and dreams on the line and opened up my wallet.

Ready for Takeoff

Words can't express how excited I was to get the website design process started. When the designer finished creating the website, I was more certain than ever that success was just around the corner.

Then, we launched the website. *Insert the sound of crickets chirping here.* Nothing happened! Yes, I mean nothing. No new business. No new phone calls. No visitors to the site. Nothing.

How was this possible? The web designer had assured me my hopes and dreams weren't unrealistic.

Reality Check—and More Money

I knew there had to be mistake. Maybe there was a button in the code that the designer forgot to click. Something! Anything!

I did the only logical thing: I called the web designer for an explanation. His answer for the inactivity? *Oh, it's gonna take some time. You can't expect traffic overnight.*

I was enraged. I fumed over his passive response to me. Couldn't he have warned me about this in our initial meeting? But he hadn't, and I was left with the only thing I could do: Wait...and wait...and wait. And you know what? All that waiting got me what I had before I had the site built. Nothing.

That's when I decided to take matters into my own hands. I became a student of Internet marketing and sales. I consumed every article and book I could find.

Every time I learned something new, I picked up the phone and called my "expert" web designer and had him make the changes. And he promptly and happily sent me a bill.

Enough Already

I'm not sure exactly what it was that pushed me over the edge, but I finally reached the point of complete frustration. So I decided to take matters into my own hands. I did the only thing I knew to do. I started learning html code.

Learning html allowed me to make changes to my own site without incurring a stack of invoices from my web designer. It also did something far more important. It gave me the freedom to experiment on my website. I was able to make changes, monitor conversion rates, make more tweaks, and monitor some more.

Although I absolutely hated coding (and still do), it provided me with newfound freedom. Both my website and my pocketbook were better for it.

About You—and Your Website

That's enough about me. Let's talk about you and your website. You're reading this book for one of two reasons:

1. You have a website—and you expect more from it.
2. You want a website—and you want to be sure it's remarkable.

If either of those describes you, then you'll benefit from this book. In this book, I hope to have a conversation with you. A conversation with three goals:

1.) Convince you that you can have a remarkable website, the kind of website that brings you closer to your goals and dreams (and helps you make a difference in the world).

2.) Help you discover some of the psychology behind what makes a website remarkable and how you can apply some of these tactics on your own site

3.) Provide you with specific, often step-by-step instructions for making small changes that will bring big results

If this is a conversation you'd like to continue, I guess there are only two things left to do. First, grab your favorite beverage (I've got my cup or coffee). Second, keep reading.

Hang On Just a Minute!

Before you invest another second of your most valuable resource, time, I want to help you determine if this book is right for you. It does me no good to have you spend the next X amount of time reading this book to reach the end and feel as if you've wasted your time.

So here's a simple test to discover if your website is reaching its full potential:

1.) Am I happy with how my website is performing right now?

2.) Is it helping me capture leads and make sales?

3.) Is this how I envisioned my level of success when I launched my website?

If you had to give your website a grade based on those three questions, what grade would you give it?

And now for the most important question:

If I told you that I was going to send five hundred qualified prospects to your website tomorrow, would you—and your website—be ready for them?

If you answered no to any or all of the questions above, then it may be time to reevaluate your online plan of action. This book was designed not only to help you reevaluate your website, but also to give you specific—actionable—steps you can begin implementing today.

Can You Handle the Truth?

If you're still reading, I'm assuming you agree that this book is for you and that it's not going to be a waste of your time. It's obvious that you're serious about getting more results from your website.

First, though, you have to promise to take action on what you learn. There's no point in spending your time reading this book if you aren't going to apply what you read. Promise me you'll take one idea that you learn from this book and apply it today. You promise? Okay, let's dive in!

The Critical 5

The first step toward getting better results from your website is to have clearly defined goals. You can just hope for more people to arrive, cross your fingers, and say a prayer, if that's what you'd prefer. But be forewarned. That usually doesn't end up working so well, despite what the media would have you believe.

That's why you need the Critical 5, a series of questions designed to help you get the most out of your website—and more. Answer the Critical 5 for each page on your website, and I guarantee you'll have a clear picture of your website's weak spots. The Critical 5 will not only help you identify your website's weak spots, but also help you craft content that both persuades your audience and generates a favorable response.

Here are the Critical 5:

1. **Who's here?**—Before crafting your message, you've got to understand who will be "listening" to

your message. Is it a prospect? Is it a customer? Is it an employee?

2. **What action should they take?**—What action do you want them to take? Contact you? Learn more? Share with friends? Complete an application?

3. **When should they do it?** When do I want them to take the action? Today, tomorrow, at some other point in the future?

4. **Why should they take it?** The visitors on your website are asking, "What's In It For Me?" WIIFM? Sorry to break the news to you, but they really don't care about you. They are interested only in meeting their needs and fulfilling their desires. Be sure you communicate *why* they should take action.

5. **How can I convince them?**—What story, or message, can you communicate to your audience to help them take the action you desire?

Take some time to review each page on your website, answering the Critical 5 for each page. It would be worth taking a few minutes *now* to review your site. Sure, it doesn't sound like fun and it does take time, but the payoff will be *huge*.

Most people discover that a few of their pages are good, but most of their pages don't do so well on the Critical 5 test. **If your website didn't do well, that's great!** No, that's not a misprint. If your website didn't do well, at least you now know where your website's weaknesses lie. The rest of this book is going to give you specific steps for improving the Critical 5 and getting amazing results from your website.

Don't Miss the Boat

The most common mistake is ignoring the second part of the Critical 5, the WHAT. Most people aren't clear about what action they want people to take.

Fortunately, correcting the WHAT for your website is often as simple as changing the text on the web page. Here's a simple formula taught by master copywriter John Carlton:

- **Tell them what you've got**—or tell them what you want them to do.

- **Tell them what it'll do for them**—or tell them why they should take the action you want them to take. (this is the WHY)

- **Tell them what to do next**—'Nough said. (this is the HOW)

Sure, those three steps sound simple, but don't let their simplicity fool you, they will make it easy for you to explain clearly what action you'd like your visitors to take and why they should take it now.

The reality is a number of people who read this book will simply dismiss the Critical Five as "something I'll worry about later." If you were to make that decision, you'd be making a horrible mistake. If you don't take anything else away from this book, you must come to the realization that understanding *and* serving your audience is the most important thing you can ever do.

Be sure you thoroughly know your audience. Over the next few pages, you'll hear examples from a few people who didn't know much when they got started—but what they did know was the importance of knowing and serving their audience. I hope their stories will encourage and inspire you to start where you are, with the resources you have.

> *"Do not wait; the time will never be 'just right.' Start where you stand, and work with whatever tools you may have at your command, and better tools will be found as you go along."*
>
> **—Napoleon Hill**

Turning a Hobby into a Profitable Business

Brian Goulet, The Goulet Pen Company

The Goulet Pen Company began as a hobby in 2007 when Brian Goulet's lifelong interest in woodworking led him to purchase a small lathe and give fountain pen making a try. Brian's pens quickly became a hit with his friends and family.

Although Brian and his wife, Rachel, were living in an apartment, and Brian's "workshop" was on their covered balcony, he picked up his first corporate order quickly, turning his hobby into a business in a matter of weeks. Brian made his pens on nights and weekends until late 2008. It was then he decided to devote his career to making custom writing instruments.

It's important to notice the way Brian successfully ignored "Yeah But Disease" as he started his business. He could have easily said,

> Yeah, but I don't have experience making custom writing instruments.
>
> Yeah, but I don't have a workshop.
>
> Yeah, but I don't have time.
>
> Yeah, but I don't know anything about the fountain pen industry.

Any of those "Yeah But Disease" thoughts could have easily killed his dreams, but Brian didn't let them. He kept pushing, and he chose to ignore those thoughts.

Expansion

Brian was eager to expand his business, but wasn't sure which direction to go in next. He turned to online fountain pen forums to see what people were saying. By observing conversations and asking a lot of questions, he was able to identify voids in the market quickly.

Once the voids were identified, the Goulet Pen Company began building a loyal following by offering products to fill those voids, having competitive prices, utilizing an educational and inspirational marketing approach through their blog *Ink Nouveau,* and providing a weekly live broadcast called *Write Time at 9.*

There are many lessons we can learn (and borrow) from Brian and Rachel's success with the Goulet Pen Company—and we will. For now, though, let's start with one of the most important questions you must answer for yourself.

How Can I Serve the Market?

Brian was serious about turning his hobby into a business, and he wanted to thoroughly understand his potential customers. He wanted to know their needs, their wants, where they shopped, how they shopped, when they shopped, and what they bought.

This is the same place you should start. Whether you're evaluating your website or your entire business, you have to understand clearly the audience you are serving. You have to know how you can both meet and exceed their expectations.

The Natural Progression

Even if you're not physically selling anything on your website, you're still selling on your website. Don't you want the visitors on your website to do business with you eventually? At least, don't you want them to read, like, and share your content?

Regardless of what industry you are in (for-profit or non-profit), all websites serve the same purpose, and that purpose is to *begin (or continue) a conversation*. Here's what the natural progression of web traffic should look like:

Stranger → Friend → Customer → Repeat Customer → Evangelist

Skipping this natural order of progression is like going out on a first date and asking the person to marry you. If you did this, the person would probably run away. The same will be true with your website if you skip this natural progression.

Signs that you may be skipping the natural progression:

- You believe visitors will make a purchase on their first visit.

- You have no mechanism specifically designed to continue the initial conversation.
- Your banner says, "BUY NOW!"
- Your site won an award for having an amazing design, so you believe no other action is required.
- You constantly pester your friends to promote your website on Facebook and Twitter.

You have to keep in mind that most people are merely browsing the Internet when they land on your website. And this is a big problem. It leaves you with three specific jobs if you're going to succeed in following the natural progression:

1. Enticing them to explore more of your website
2. Getting them to come back to your website
3. Continuing the conversation even after they've left

Unfortunately, most web designers leave these three crucial jobs to the owner of the website. Designers ignore them because they assume it has nothing to do with design. They're wrong! Natural progression has *everything* to do with design.

"It's not creative unless it sells."

—**David Ogilvy**

Great website design has little to do with creativity and great visual appeal. *Great design has everything to do with how the website will begin and continue conversations with visitors.*

That last sentence is worth reading again. Beginning and continuing conversations is the true essence of what a website does. Sounds simple (and it is). But you have to be willing to devote time, energy, and effort to the conversation.

The scalability of websites is what makes them such potentially powerful tools. They give you the ability to begin and continue conversations with thousands (even millions) of people at the same time.

Brian Goulet began his company and online business with conversations. His journey began by reading and starting conversations with others on forums. It's these conversations that eventually spilled over to his blog.

Getting Them to Explore

Single-sentence conversations don't go very far toward building relationships. Single-sentence conversations are what occur when someone visits only one page on your website and then leaves. If they're visiting only one page, it's really difficult to build a relationship.

If you're not committed to building relationships, your visitors will never trust you. If they don't trust you, they won't take the action you want them to take. If they don't take the action you want them to take, they certainly won't become evangelists helping to spread your message.

Although it may seem like a complex problem, the solution is quite simple: create longer conversations. This can be done simply by enticing them to explore more of your website. This movement of the visitor through the pages of your website is called *site-flow*. You want great site-flow so visitors will flow through the pages of your site. This will help motivate them to build a relationship, gain trust in you and your organization, and spend more time on your website.

The first time a visitor lands on your website is like a first date, and your goal is to get the second date. You certainly won't get the second date if you screw up the first.

Fortunately, there are only three ways to screw up the first date with your visitors:

- Ask them for a long-term relationship too soon.
- Bore them.
- Offend them.

Carefully evaluating your website with the Critical 5 will enable you to be a better first date. Let's assume that you're sufficiently prepared for your first date, and now it's time to ask for the second date.

Getting Them to Come Back

Think for a minute about your favorite websites. I'm talking about those you visit regularly. Picture each one in your mind. What keeps you coming back? Write down a few reasons.

Now, all the reasons you jotted down likely contain one or a combination of the following four elements:

- **Needs**—They provide something (products, services, advice, and/or content) that meets your needs. (Maybe it's a site you have to reference regularly for your job.)
- **Desires**—They provide something that fulfills some of your desires. (Maybe your passion is gardening, and they provide great gardening info, photos, videos, etc.)

- **Entertainment**—They provide something that entertains you. (Facebook, People.com, YouTube.com, etc.)
- **Necessity**—You have to visit their website out of necessity. (Maybe you pay your bills, check your account balance, or view the status of something.)

Into which of these four categories does *your* website fit? If it doesn't fit into any category at this point, into which category do you believe would be the easiest to transition your website?

> Ask yourself, "If I visited my website, would I have a compelling reason to return?"

One of the simplest ways to get people to return to your website is to continue the conversation with them once they've left your website.

Continue the Conversation

The most frequented websites in the world provide a method of continuing the conversation—even when people aren't on the website. There are several ways to accomplish this, but each involves engaging your audience in a meaningful way. Most notably, all involve some mechanism of *gaining permission to continue the conversation.*

Often the simplest way to continue the conversation is through *lead capture.* Lead capture is a method of collecting some variation of contact information from the visitors on your website. You can collect as little or as much information as you believe is necessary to continue the conversation successfully. (You'll discover that most websites collect only a name and e-mail address.)

> **Key point:** The more information you ask for, the fewer people will provide their info (a.k.a. opt-in). For example, if all you ask for is an e-mail address, you'll typically have a higher percentage of visitors provide this than if you ask for both their name and e-mail address.

The flip side is the more information you request from your visitors, the more qualified the person will be. For example, if someone is willing to provide you with his or her name, e-mail address, phone number, and mailing address, there is a decent chance he or she is interested in what you're offering.

You'll discover there is often a direct correlation between the perceived value of what you're offering and the amount of information people are willing to provide. For example, you may have opted-in to receive this book by providing only your name and e-mail address. On the other hand, if I were offering to give you a ten-thousand-dollar marketing course, you would likely be willing to provide a lot more information.

Why?

Because there's a lot more value (whether perceived or real) in the ten-thousand-dollar marketing course. So, what's of value to your audience? Brian Goulet's audience wanted to know how to learn more about the best journals and writing instruments. In both cases, they each took the time to discover the needs of their audiences. It's only after you discover your audience's needs, wants, and desires that you are able to adequately serve them through your website.

The Texas Two-Step

No, I'm not referring to the dance. I'm referring to the two simple steps required to build a list of followers that look forward to hearing from you.

Step 1—Enticement Tool

You need an enticement tool that can be used to begin a conversation with your visitors. This enticement tool has to be compelling enough that people are willing to provide you with their contact information in exchange.

An example of an enticement tool would be this book. Because you were willing to exchange your name and e-mail address for this book, I can make a few assumptions about you:

- You have a website.
- You are considering getting a website.

- You are a competitor and want to see what I'm up to with this book.

But honestly it doesn't matter which (if any) of those assumptions is true, and here's why: natural progression. I don't care why you opted in to get this book, but I'm honored that you have decided to allow me to start and continue a conversation with you.

Keys to Enticement

Here are a few questions to help ensure that your enticement tool truly entices:

> **What are your audience's needs or desires?** You want to be sure your "enticement" matches these.
>
> **What can you offer them that will help them get closer to meeting their needs or fulfilling their desires?** Would your audience benefit from a special report? A video? A conference call? A webinar?
>
> **What small actionable steps can you provide them that will help them get one step closer to their goal?** The first person I know who successfully used this principle on a mass scale was Dale Carnegie. (I highly recommend Dale's book *How to Win Friends and Influence People*.)

Over seventy years ago, Dale Carnegie started teaching classes at the YMCA on "How to Win Friends and Influence People." Unfortunately (or fortunately), Dale was paid based only on the number of people who attended the weekly course. To ensure people would keep coming back week after week, each week

Dale gave his students one simple assignment to implement prior to the next class. The key was that simple assignment provided the student with immediate visual results.

I've done the same thing in this book. I've provided dozens of small actionable steps that you can immediately implement and see results from. If you're not seeing results from these steps, chances are you're not implementing what you're learning.

Okay, so now you should have a good idea of what you can use as an enticement tool. Now it's time for step two.

Step 2—Capture Them

You'll need an opt-in form on your website to capture and store your visitors' contact info. Unless you plan on manually sending your enticement tool to each person who requests it, it would be good to utilize an autoresponder.

An autoresponder is software that automatically responds when an e-mail is sent to it.

If you signed up to receive this book on our website (UglyMugMarketing.com), you received it through our autoresponder. (For those who are curious, the name of our autoresponder is Aweber.com.)

When someone provides the required information and hits the "Submit" button, your autoresponder automatically begins the predefined sequence that you establish.

Don't worry; setting up an autoresponder isn't as difficult as it may sound. There are several companies that provide e-mail management and autoresponder services for very reasonable rates. At the time of this writing, MailChimp.com offers a free account if you have less than 2,500 people who have opted in. Here are some other companies that provide autoresponder service:

    Aweber.com
    ConstantContact.com
    IContact.com
    GetResponse.com

At this point, there is no need to spend much time analyzing autoresponders. Each of the ones we mentioned will do a great job, and each is easy to use. All provide very helpful tutorials for how to get started setting up your autoresponder.

So, by now you hopefully know *who* your website visitors are, and you've given them clear instruction on *what* to do next. That's two of the Critical 5. With a fairly solid foundation in place, it's time to start getting more people to your website.

But What If I'm All Alone?
My website isn't getting any traffic

Building an Online Empire
With Chris Guillebeau

Chris Guillebeau isn't your ordinary blogger, but he is your ordinary *successful* blogger. It hasn't always been this way. He struggled. He wrote a lot (a thousand words a day, seven days a week). He studied. He made mistakes. He learned. He made changes. And finally—after 279 days—he succeeded.

Chris's passions are traveling, living a life of nonconformity, and sharing his experiences with others through his blog http://chrisguillebeau.com/3x5/.

Chris's online journey began with study and lots of writing. He started by spending an entire year studying what the most successful bloggers were (and weren't) doing. While carefully watching and studying others, he kept busy writing (and rewriting).

Not only did Chris launch his blog, but he also released a manifesto entitled, *A Brief Guide to World Domination*. However, releasing a manifesto without an audience is like screaming in a forest—no one is gonna hear you. Once he had his manifesto ready, he began sending it to people and asking for feedback and suggestions on how he could improve it.

The key isn't in asking for feedback, but in implementing the changes based on the feedback. *A Brief Guide to World Domination* has now been downloaded over 100,000 times, reviewed by over 400 bloggers, and commented on over 500 times on Chris's blog. Most important, it became a catalyst for Chris's online success.

His manifesto is also a tool Chris used to continue the conversation with readers once they have left his website. Throughout his manifestos (he currently has three, and all are worth reading), Chris has links that point people back to various articles and other posts on his website. These links provide people with easy points of return to his website.

No Product—No Problem

When Chris released his first manifesto (and launched his blog), he didn't have any products or services for sale. Nothing! He had a plan, though, and he understood that he could have everything he wanted by helping other people get what they wanted.

> *"You can have everything in life you want if you're willing to help enough other people get what they want."*
>
> **—Zig Ziglar**

Chris was passionate not only about sharing his story, but also about helping others to become more successful. So he wrote. And wrote. And wrote. And then he wrote some more. These were not just fluff blog posts. He produced (and still produces) some amazing content each and every week, and he gave it all away on his blog.

Although it seems a little crazy to give away such great content, Chris wasn't concerned because he understood the natural progression of web traffic. If you understand the natural progression of web traffic, you will be able to remain calm when it seems like you're screaming in the forest.

You can have the best offer in the world, but it is useless if nobody knows about it. So, where is the best place to start? Before you start generating traffic to your website, you need to have an analytics program monitoring your website.

> **An analytics program** allows you to measure where and how traffic flows through your website.

Without some form of analytics software, you won't be able to see how visitors are flowing through your website. You also won't be able to determine if the changes and tweaks you are making on your website are working. There are several companies that provide great analytics software, but the one I recommend you start with is Google Analytics.

Google Analytics will measure everything from the number of visitors to specifically which pages they viewed—and even which page they were on when they left your site. There is so much more to it, too. The best part of all is that Google Analytics is free.

You can sign up for your free account here: http://www.google.com/analytics/ Installing Google Analytics is as simple as copying and pasting one small section of code. Once you have it installed, you will be able to start tracking traffic patterns on your website.

The Basics of Generating Traffic

So, now it's time for us to start generating some traffic to your website. The first place we need to begin is by understanding the three different places you can get website traffic.

1. **Paid traffic** is traffic that you pay for. It could be from a banner ad, text ad, link ad, affiliate link, or any other traffic that you pay to receive.

2. **Organic traffic** is traffic you receive from search engines. You receive this traffic without directly paying for it. (This is what good Search Engine Optimization, or SEO, can provide. More on that late.)

3. **Offline traffic** is website traffic you receive as a result of your offline marketing/advertising activities.

Don't allow the seemingly hundreds of options for generating traffic overwhelm you. They all fall into one of three places mentioned above. We'll start with the sources that can provide you the quickest traffic.

Get Traffic Now

All this reading and preparing to build your web empire is great, but enough already. Let's get some traffic to your website—fast. How fast? How about within the next couple of hours? It's really not as difficult as you might expect. Some of these solutions are so simple that most people simply overlook them.

> **WARNING: Don't start sending more traffic to your website until you've complete the Critical 5 (see the introduction).**

Each of the following methods is effective at generating traffic to your website. However, you'll likely find that using several of these at the same time will provide you with synergy and generate more traffic. We'll start with the simplest and work to the most difficult. (None of these steps is very difficult; it's just that some require a little more time.)

1. **E-mail signature**—People are often surprised by how much traffic they start generating by simply

adding a link to their website in their e-mail signature. All of the largest e-mail services provide the ability to customize the signature that appears on the bottom of your e-mail messages. (Not sure how? Simply do a Google search for "adding an e-mail signature in _____." Insert the name of your e-mail service provider in the blank.)

If you want extra credit, try making special offers in your e-mail signature. For example you could write, "Save 25 percent off our widgets this weekend only." Then make that entire sentence point to a web page that promotes your special discount.

2. **E-mail**—Send an e-mail to all your contacts, telling them to check out your website. Or better yet, send them a special offer for being a friend, family member, etc. (Don't spam. Only e-mail people who have given you permission to e-mail them. And don't become that annoying friend or family member that continually pushes their products and services on others.)

3. **Social media**—Utilize Facebook, Twitter, and LinkedIn to let others know that you've made changes to your website. Keep in mind that they are tuned in to WIIFM (What's In It For Me). Be sure you tell them why they'll benefit from checking out your website.

4. **Leverage others**—Have a friend with a website? What about a friend with e-mail contacts? Great! Buy them lunch in exchange for mentioning your website to their

contacts (or linking from their website to yours). (Again, don't spam, and don't ask others to spam for you.)

5. **Be a good guest**—If you know someone with a blog, offer to write a blog post for their blog. Here are a few tips for getting others to allow you to write a guest post:
    a. **Keep it relevant.** Be sure to write about things their readers are interested in reading.
    b. **Don't sell.** Don't use your guest post to sell. Use your guest post to generate traffic. Do this by really impressing the readers with your content and then linking to your website in a brief footer bio.
    c. **Return the favor.** Make your audience available to your friends. Offer to promote them and their products or services to your audience.

6. **Offline marketing.** At a minimum, be sure all your offline marketing and print materials provide your web address. If you want to be more aggressive, use offline marketing to channel and funnel prospects through your website.

    Using offline marketing to drive web traffic is probably one of the most overlooked traffic generating methods. Grab a copy of any business related magazine (Inc., Forbes, Fast Company, etc.) and you will likely find several web-based companies advertising their services. Although you probably can't afford space in one of these national magazines, you can afford space in local or regional publications.

7. **Pay per click (PPC)**—With PPC, you pay only when someone clicks your ad and goes to your website (or a specific page on your website). Pay-per-click can be one of the most effective forms of marketing and traffic generating. The reason is simple: you are only paying for traffic that ends up on your site.

    I recommend starting with Google AdWords. Why? They make it easy to set up, and they are still by far the largest search engine in the world. We'll jump into exactly how to set up a Google pay-per-click campaign a little later.

8. **Get press.** Utilizing press and publicity is another great way to generate immediate traffic to your website. I know, I know, you may not have a clue where to start or what to do to get publicity. The great news is you don't have to. There are companies that can handle all of this for you for a small fee.

    PRWeb.com and PRLeap.com are two of the most popular, and both would be worth familiarizing yourself with. Either can handle writing, publishing, and distributing your press release for as little as forty-nine dollars.

Quick Review—Where Are We?

Let's do a quick review. First we started by laying the proper foundation—getting your website ready for traffic (the Critical 5). Next we began the process of getting traffic to your website. All of these things are great, but now we need to turn our focus to long-term strategies. These strategies will continually send traffic to your website.

But First, Action Is Required

Reading this book is great. Honestly, I'm flattered that you've already spent this much time reading something that I've written. But if you start taking action based on the information found in this book, I will be ecstatic.

> *"You see, in life, lots of people know what to do, but few people actually do what they know. Knowing is not enough! You must take action."*
>
> **- Anthony Robbins**

Look back over the eight simple ideas and pick one. Now stop reading and go do the step you picked.

Long-Term Traffic Strategies

It's a great feeling to simply send out an e-mail or to make a Facebook post and immediately start getting traffic to your website. Want to know what's an even better feeling? Getting visitors to your site day after day without any new effort on your part.

There are certain strategies that, once implemented, will continually send traffic to your website. These aren't some lofty or ridiculous ideas. No, all of these ideas are tried and true. And best of all, they work.

So let's get going.

Strategy 1—Give Them a Reason to Return

Think for a minute about your favorite websites. You know, the ones that you go back to over and over again.

I'd be willing to bet that all of the sites you visit on a regular basis have one thing in common: fresh new content. Right?

You wouldn't want to go to a website if it was the same thing over and over again. One of my favorites is Amazon. What I love most about Amazon is "discovering" new books that I haven't read. In many cases, I find books I've never even heard of.

Amazon does this through a feature they call "Recommended for You." If I'm looking at a new marketing book from Seth Godin, Amazon recommends additional books that may be of interest to me. Although the majority of the books they recommend for me have been out for a while, they are new to me. This web feature keeps me interested and engaged.

Now let's talk about your website. What compelling reason are you giving prospects and clients to come back and visit your site again? If you can't think of any, chances are pretty good that your website isn't getting much repeat traffic. Let's look at a few ways you can get visitors to come back.

Getting Repeat Visitors

If you want people to come back, you must provide them with a "new" experience each time they visit. Think Amazon. Their website design stays the same each time I visit (and has for years), but each time I'm on their website, it's a completely unique experience. This is because of their recommendations.

So, how can you keep people coming back with a limited budget? Here are a few techniques:

- **Rotate inventory**—Move your inventory around the site. Change the inventory that is displayed on your home page.

- **Rotate content**—Move your content from page to page. Keep visitors wondering what will happen next.
- **Release new inventory**—Consider releasing new products or services regularly. Let visitors know when to expect new inventory.
- **Release new content**—A blog is a great way to release new content regularly.
- **Allow user-generated content**—Allow users to post reviews and comments. This will create a continual cycle of new content.
- **Allow users to interact**—Slides, videos, and audio are all great ways to make your website a multisensory experience.
- **Interact with users**—Let your visitors know you appreciate their attention and time. Give them tools to communicate directly to you.
- **Entertain people**—Make your website a fun place to visit.
- **Don't reveal everything**—Let users "discover" things through your website. Don't make all your content and inventory obvious.
- **Invite participation**—Let your visitors know you want them to participate in the content and conversation.

Strategy 2—Write Articles

Write articles to publish on other websites *for free*. Sound crazy? When I was first advised to write for free, I thought it was a ridiculous idea, but now I'll be the first to *highly* recommend it. Here are three reasons why it's important.

- **Market penetration**—Publishing articles on other websites allows you to spread your message to an audience that may not have heard about you or your message before.
- **Backlink(s)**—In exchange for having your article published on another website, you'll typically receive a link(s) pointing back to your website. Backlinks are very important when it comes to Search Engine Optimization—which we'll discuss in more detail shortly.
- **Credibility**—When you start referencing the sites to which you contribute, it helps build your credibility as an "expert" in your field.

Places to Publish Your Article

There are numerous places you can publish your articles online. All the places I recommend are completely free. Here are a few of those places:

- Squidoo.com
- Hubpages.com
- Ezinearticles.com
- Gather.com
- Goarticles.com
- Brighthub.com
- Buzzle.com

The disadvantage of publishing your work on article directories is that your article is only one of thousands that appear on the site. In many cases your article simply disappears into cyberspace.

Despite this flaw, there are still several reasons you should consider publish your articles on these directories.

> **Backlinks**—The majority of the articles directories mentioned above give you the ability to add links pointing back to your website. It's often said that links are the currency of the Internet, so this benefit alone can be extremely valuable.
>
> **Credibility**—In case you haven't noticed, the Internet is the land of self-proclaimed "gurus." The Internet has the Internet to claim to be an expert. Because of this guru trend, online users are becoming more and more skeptical. By publishing some of your articles on an articles directory, you can reference your published work on the directories to help demonstrate your "guru" status and build some credibility.

Better Than Article Directories

Article directories are great, but doing guest blog posts on other blogs can (and more than likely will) provide you with far better results. Yes, guest blog posts are just what they sound like: publishing an article/post on another blogger's website. Let's look at some of the benefits of guest blogging, and then we'll go over very specific steps for getting other bloggers to allow you to do a guest post:

Instant credibility—To the blogger's audience, you have instant credibility. It's implied that if the blogger trusts you enough to be a guest author, then his or her audience should trust you as well.

Expanded reach—By publishing content on another person's blog, you are exposing yourself and your message to an audience that you may not have otherwise reached.

Contextual authority—If you were to do a guest post on my blog, MarketingConfessions.com, my audience would automatically assume that you must be an authority in one of the core areas I write about on my blog. After all, why else would I allow someone who is not an authority to post on my blog?

Backlinks—Often bloggers will allow you to provide a backlink pointing back to your website. These links alone can prove to be a very valuable tool for generating traffic to your website.

Six Steps to Becoming a Guest Blogger

1. **Build your previous work.** I'll be honest; this is the step most people don't like to hear. Not because it's difficult, but because it takes time. Before you begin reaching out to other bloggers, I recommend you spend at least three to six months building up your own content. This will give the blogger for whom you're hoping to blog something to review to determine if you would be a good match for their audience. And it shows them that you aren't a newbie.

2. **Know their audience.** I'm sure you've heard the ancient Greek saying, "Know Thyself." Well, when it comes to being a guest blogger, you can throw it out the window and instead use "Know Them."

   When you are guest blogging, it is crucial that you know each blog's audience. You need to know why they read that particular blog. You also need to know to what type(s) of blog posts they respond to the best. Here are a few ways to help you determine which posts the blog's audience responds to most favorably:

   - Number of comments
   - Quality of the comments
   - Number of shares on social media
   - Number of times the blogger has published similar content

By taking some time to review the blogger's past posts, you'll be able to gain a pretty clear idea as to what his or her audience will like most.

3. **Know their approach.** Learning how they position themselves and how they approach their audience is easy to determine. Typically, you can figure this out simply by looking at their "About" page. Start by taking a look at what is there (the content) and how it is presented (the style):

   - How are they attempting to position themselves?
   - In what style is the page written?

Most bloggers position themselves in one of the following ways:

- Unapproachable expert
- Approachable expert
- Average guy just sharing his experiences

Without question, you can become a guest blogger for any of these types. However, the "approachable expert" will typically be the easiest avenue to take for getting a favorable response.

4. **Casually ask the blogger.** Bloggers—yes, even super successful bloggers—are just regular people. You shouldn't be afraid to ask them to let you guest post, but you should do it in a casual way. Here's an example:

"Hi, John,

I hope you're having a great week!

I've been following your blog for several months now, and I'm always amazed by the great content that you publish each week. I'm a marketing executive, so I particularly enjoy your posts on creative advertising techniques. Here are a couple of my favorite posts:

www.sample—blog.com/marketing—that—works
www.sample—blog.com/marketing—magic

I also blog over at www.myfakeblog.com on a variety of marketing topics. I know that you don't publish many posts by guest authors, but I have a post that I really believe your readers may enjoy. It's titled "30 Creative Marketing Techniques."

I've attached a copy of the posts as well as the html version, should you decide to use it. You know your audience better than anyone, so feel free to edit the post however you see fit.

I'm sure you stay extremely busy, so I completely understand if you don't have time to consider using my post.

Thanks again for all the great content you publish each week. Let me know if there is anything I can ever do to help you.

Best regards,
Wayne Mullins

You can see that this approach is very casual and unassuming. It gives the blogger an easy way out if he or she doesn't like your post. If bloggers don't respond, wait another week and send a very polite and casual reminder. If they still don't, move on to the next opportunity.

5. **Deliver as promised.** Don't be alarmed or offended if the blogger responds asking you to make edits or adjustments to your post. They know what their audience likes, so make the changes requested. Do it quickly. Don't delay. If you tell them you'll send back revisions within two hours, be sure you send back revisions within two hours. No later.

6. **Show gratitude.** Regardless, if the blogger accepts or declines your guest post, show them gratitude. If your post is accepted, you know what to say; but if your post is rejected, still let them know how much you appreciate

and enjoy the content they publish. Let them know how you've specifically benefited from what you've learned on their blog.

It's Going to Happen

You will be told no. And that's completely normal—and okay. Don't let this deter you. I'm not going to lie; getting your pitch to guest blog rejected isn't easy to take. If you're anything like me, this no will cause you to second guess your decision to guest post—and maybe even your decision to blog. Don't lose heart, though. Instead, simply move on to the next person on your list.

While you're reaching out and connecting with others, it's a good idea to start thinking about the other opportunities that could arise from building relationships with these people.

Strategy 3—Online Networking

The web is really like one ginormous Chamber of Commerce networking event. It has never been easier to reach out and connect with others, but it's also never been easier to ruin potentially rewarding relationships. The key to successful online networking is to take a strategic approach before connecting with online influencers.

Here are a few places and ways you can network on the web:
- a. **Joint ventures**—Find others with an audience similar to yours, but who don't have directly competing products. Agree to promote their products or services in exchange for them promoting yours.

b. **Affiliate marketing**—Affiliate marketing is similar to joint ventures, with the primary difference being that money is typically exchanged in return for a sale. (This is explored in a little more detail below.)
   c. **Serve others**—Don't be the guy or gal who always has your hand out wanting something. Instead be the one who is always serving others in your online "community." Before you ask someone for a favor, remember they are tuned in to WIIFM (What's In It For Me).

Affiliate Marketing

There are several online affiliate marketplaces. These are places where you can find people looking to promote products as well as find products to promote. Clickbank.com is the largest and best website for finding digital products. Jounce.com is a great place for physical products.

One of the products I sell online is an e-book on how to start and grow a lawn business. I use Clickbank.com to find my affiliates. When one of my affiliates sends someone to my website and they purchase my book, the affiliate is rewarded with a commission on that sale.

Strategy 4—Newsletter Publishing

This is my personal favorite. A simple newsletter can keep current clients up-to-date on what's happening as well as keep your name at the forefront of your prospect's minds.

I actively used newsletters in a previous business. That business experienced at 300 percent growth rate for three consecutive years. We actively use newsletters at Ugly Mug Marketing, and we have experienced a very similar growth rate.

Here are a few things to consider including in your newsletter:

    a. **Actionable advice**—Provide some specific, *relevant* advice that your clients can immediately implement.

    b. **Data**—Give sales data, number of clients, working projects, and anything else that helps build your credibility.

    c. **Call to action**—Your newsletter needs to have a clear call to action. Tell the readers exactly what they should do next and why they'll benefit from doing it.

    d. **Testimonials**—There's no better way to build credibility. Have people talk about what they experienced from working with you and your business.

    e. **Client profiles**—Consider featuring one of your "best" clients in your newsletter. This provides a lot of goodwill between you and your client, and it provides a great way to "borrow" your client's credibility.

There are many services online that provide easy-to-build online newsletter templates. My personal favorites are MailChimp and Aweber.

Strategy 5—Get Links, a.k.a. Backlinks

Work on getting other websites to link to your website. We'll cover more about getting links in the Search Engine Optimization section.

Strategy 6—Foster Referrals and Sharing

Both can be summed up in the phrase "word of mouth." Look at your site through the eyes of a visitor, and then ask yourself, "Is there anything here that I would want to share with my friends?" If not, what could you add that would be worthy of sharing with others? Here are some ideas:

a. **Reward referrals**—Give your visitors an incentive for referring others. You may be able to offer a special discount or access to a member's only area for visitors whom refer others to your website.

b. **Make it easy**—Make it easy for others to share on Facebook and Twitter. If you're using WordPress, take a look at adding the Sharebar and Share This plugins.

c. **Let them know**—Getting your visitors to share and refer others may be as easy as letting your visitors know you expect them to share or refer, and that doing this is normal on your website.

Strategy 7—Search Engine Optimization

Way too much to cover here. See the Search Engine Optimization section.

Strategy 8—Video

YouTube.com is now the second-largest search engine on the web (behind Google). Video is quickly becoming the most consumed form of media on the web. It's now easier than ever for businesses to utilize video to generate online traffic.

Brian Goulet is a master of using video to drive traffic and ultimately sales to his website. I was first introduced to Brian after doing a search for a Moleskine journal review. I stumbled across a comparison video (http://youtu.be/LqCCyNMW7do) in which he was examining a Moleskine journal and a Rhodia journal.

That one simple video led me to purchase my first Rhodia journal from Goulet Pens; and because of Brian's exceptional marketing, I've since ordered over a half-dozen times from him.

When considering video, most people become paralyzed with fear. They don't know what to say. They don't know what to do. They don't know how to edit. The list grows with excuses. Brian had many of those same fears when he began using video, but he didn't let those fears prevent him from taking action.

Here are a few resources:

   a. **Camera**—You can obtain a good-quality HD camera for less than two hundred dollars. Here are a couple of my favorites:

- i. **Flip UltraHD**—you can get it on Amazon.com for about $130.
- ii. **Kodak Zi8**—you can get it on Amazon.com for less than $150.

b. **Where to share**—There are a lot of places online you can share your video. Here are some of the most popular:
- i. Youtube.com
- ii. Google.com/Video
- iii. Vimeo.com
- iv. Viddler.com
- v. Facebook.com

Strategy 9—Better Design

If you tell me you provide high-quality products or services, yet your website looks like it was built in 1995, I will question your claim about high-quality products or services.

Get Going!

Again, I can't stress enough the importance of getting started. Pick any one of the strategies above and begin working on it. I realize you may still have many unanswered questions, but please don't let that stop you from taking action. You can learn and get answers along the way, but the key to success is in taking action—daily.

Search Engine Optimization (SEO)

So, you sell blue widgets. Wouldn't it be wonderful if every time someone did a Google search for "blue widgets," they saw your website at the very top—ahead of all your competitors? That's the goal of search engine optimization.

The advantages to being displayed at the top of search results can be huge. I guess, in some ways, it holds the same allure as winning the lottery. Most people don't think they'll win, but they *know* they can't win if they don't play. The same is true for SEO. The odds of landing on the first page of search results are slim for many, but if you don't work on SEO, you can almost be certain you won't get on there.

How Search Engines Work

Before we jump into the basics of SEO, we first need to talk about how search engines work. Here are a few terms with which you'll need to familiarize yourself.

Spiders—Search engines have automated programs called spiders that use the hyperlink (http://en.wikipedia.org/wiki/Hyperlink) structure to "crawl" the pages that make up the web.

Indexing—After a web page has been crawled, the page contents can be "indexed." This simply means the contents are stored in a giant database.

Processing search—When someone conducts a search online, the search engine searches and sorts through all of this data (which it has indexed) and provides a search listing. All of this searching and sorting happens in a fraction of a second after someone clicks the "Search" button.

Keywords/keyword phrase—This is the word or words that someone types in the search box on a search engine.

For example, if I need a blue widget, I may do a search for "blue widget" or "discount blue widget" or "high quality blue widget." Each of those is a keyword phrase.

SO YOU HAVE A WEBSITE NOW WHAT 45

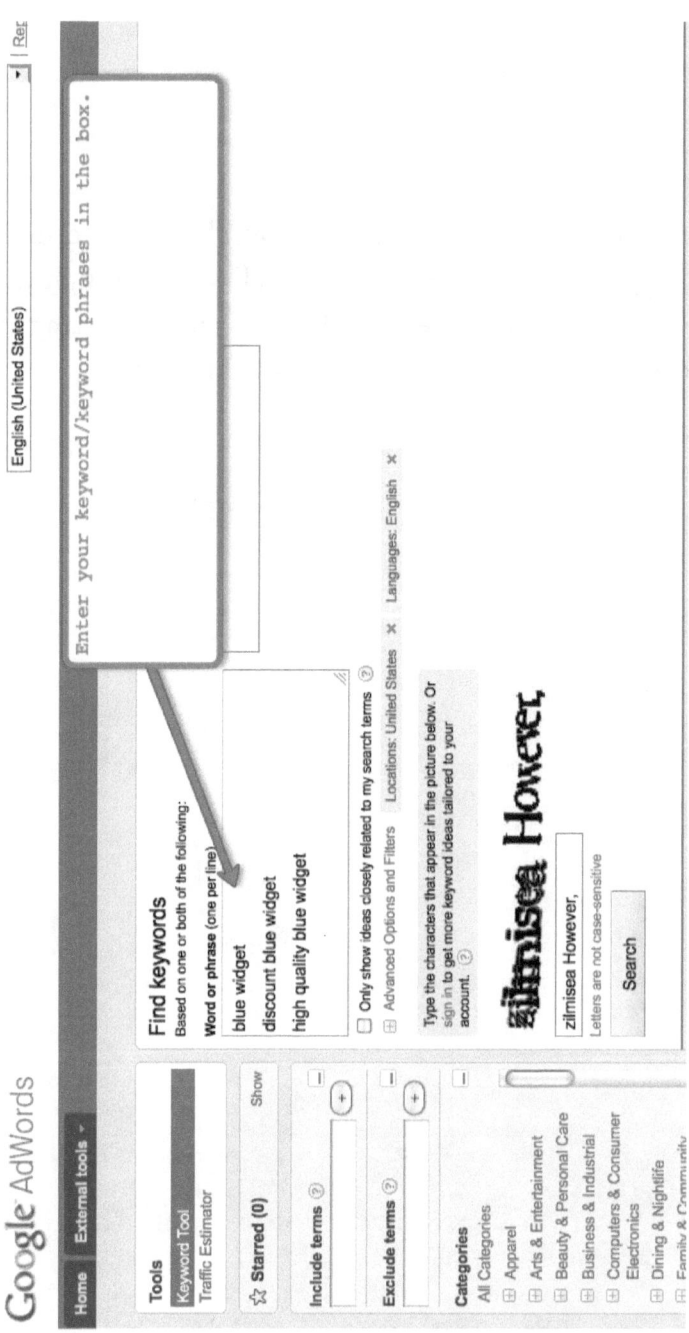

You'll notice that there were just over ninety-two million search results for those keywords. Google sorts through all the indexed pages and documents and then displays a listing of all the pages with the word *blue* and the word *widget.*

SO YOU HAVE A WEBSITE NOW WHAT 47

Google

"blue widget"   ✕ Search
                    Advanced search

About 92,500 results (0.23 seconds)

Notice the quotation marks

Notice how many fewer search results where found.

Everything
Images
Videos
News
Shopping
Discussions
More

Alexandria, LA
Change location

All results
Sites with images
More search tools

'blue widget' and 'bluewidget' Google AdWords forum at WebmasterWorld
Feb 18, 2005 ... My answer based on reading the patient research by Syzygy would lead me to answer that only "**blue-widget**" would lead to a match. ...
www.webmasterworld.com/forum81/4673.htm - Similar

Does the site have duplicate, overlapping, or redundant articles ...
Keyword better like "**blue widget**" or "blue" and "widget"? Keyword ...
"Buy blue widgets" or "**blue widget** sales." Keyword Discussion ...
"**blue widgets** online" ranking #1 "**blue widget** online" not ranking ...
More results from webmasterworld.com »

▸ WordPress › Cool-er-Sky-Blue-Widget « WordPress Plugins
Apr 2, 2010 ... Once the plugin is enabled, the widget will be available in your widgets list as "Cool-er Sky **Blue Widget**". You can add this widget to ...
wordpress.org/extend/plugins/cool-er-sky-blue-widget/ - Cached

Blue Widgets – Google and CSS Files - Graywolf's SEO Blog
If the text in the image said "large **blue widget**" then you'd be ok. Now what happens when you use a photo or illustration and not a textual image? ...
www.wolf-howl.com › Google - Cached - Similar

Blue Widget | Facebook
Blue Widget is on Facebook. Join Facebook to connect with **Blue Widget** and others you may know. Facebook gives people the power to share and makes the world ...
www.facebook.com/people/Blue-Widget/100001838153410 - Cached

SEO anchor text phrases "**blue widget**" "widget tool" vs. "**blue** ...
Nov 23, 2009 ... Question for SEOers. I have two high traffic two word phrases and a low traffic three word phrase that contains both the high traffic two ...
www.warriorforum.com/.../147934-search-engine-optimization-anchor-text-phrases-blue-widget-widget-tool-vs-blue-widget-tool.html - Cached

One Widget Two Widget Red Widget **Blue Widget** - economics consumer ...

Now let's see what happens when we do an exact phrase match.

By adding the quotation marks around the keyword phrase, we are telling Google that you want only results that contain that exact phrase. You'll notice how the search results dropped from fifty-six million to under one hundred thousand.

SO YOU HAVE A WEBSITE NOW WHAT

The keyword phrase → blue widget

The number of search results and the time it took to retrieve the list. → About 56,200,000 results (0.23 seconds)

Google

- Everything
- Images
- Videos
- News
- Shopping
- More

Alexandria, LA
Change location

All results
Sites with images
More search tools

BlueWidgets.com
No one knows for sure what **blue widgets** are, but if you're on this page there's a good chance you're a webmaster. Here are some links that will help you ...
www.bluewidgets.com/ - Cached - Block all www.bluewidgets.com results

Search Engine Optimization
Main Menu. Dirty **Blue Widgets** – SEO Podcasts Robot Stays - Privacy Policy. Categories. seo (184); SEO Suchmaschinenoptimierung Essen (1); shopping in essen ...
academyseocompetition.com/ - Cached - Similar

Blue Widgets – Google and CSS Files - Graywolf's SEO Blog
<a href="**blue-widgets**.html"><img src="images/**blue-widgets**-nav.jpg" alt="**blue widgets**">**blue widgets**</a> ...
www.wolf-howl.com › Google - Cached - Similar

"**blue widget**" and "bluewidget" Google AdWords forum at WebmasterWorld
Feb 18, 2005 ... My answer based on reading the patient research done by Syzygy would lead me to answer that only "**blue-widget**" would lead to a match. ...
www.webmasterworld.com/forum81/4673.htm - Similar

Keyword better like "**blue widget**" or "blue" and "widget"? Keyword
blue widget vs. bluewidget how does google differentiate? Google
"Buy **blue widgets**" or "**Blue widget** sales." Keyword Discussion
blue widgets online" ranking #1 "**blue widget** online" not ranking.....
More results from webmasterworld.com »

My Gadgets Review | Just another WordPress weblog
This is an example of a WordPress page, you could edit this to put information about yourself or your site so readers know where you are coming from. ...
mygadgetsreview.com/ - Cached - Similar

WordPress › Cool-er-Sky-Blue-Widget « WordPress Plugins
Apr 2, 2010 .... Once the plugin is enabled, the widget will be available in your widgets list as "Cool-er Sky **Blue Widget**". You can add this widget to ...

Keywords

Keywords are one of the fundamental pieces to SEO. You have to have a good grasp of the keywords that your potential clients would use when searching for the products or services your business provides.

Step 1

Make a list of at least ten keywords or phrases that you believe your prospects would type into Google or any other search engine when searching for the product or service that you provide.

Step 2

Now that you have a list of keywords, it's time to do some keyword research. There are several tools you can use online: Keywordspy.com, WordTracker.com, and Google Keyword Tool. My favorite—probably because it's free—is the Google Keyword Tool, so the following screen shots will be taken from there:

The information on the above slides will give you a really good idea about the results from your search. Based on our keyword "blue widget," I know that globally there are only about one thousand searches.

What would this mean for you if you sold blue widgets? It would mean that the best-case scenario is that you would reach all one thousand people with your message and product—but this is very unlikely.

SO YOU HAVE A WEBSITE NOW WHAT 51

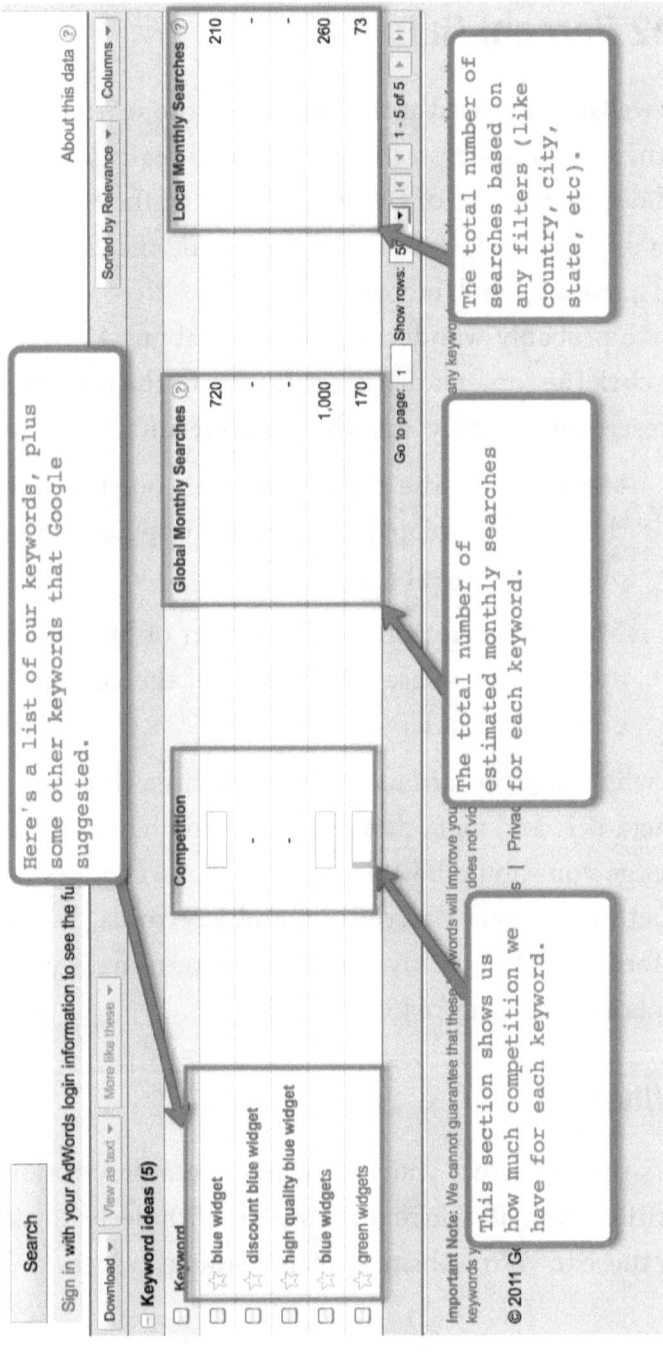

The 42 Percent Rule

If your website appeared at the very top of the search engine results (the number-one position) you could realistically expect only about 42 percent of the total search traffic to click your link. In our blue widget example, this would mean you expect around 420 clicks each month.

You're probably wondering why only about 42 percent of people click the top link. It's partially due to the meta title and meta description display with the search results.

> **Meta Title**—The portion of html code that specifics the title of a webpage. It typically appears in the tab of your Internet browser.
>
> **Meta Description**—The portion of html code that provides a concise description of the content found on that particular webpage.

This is why it's important to spend some time thinking about your meta title and meta description. If you have a little html knowledge you should be able to easily make changes to both your meta title, meta description, and keywords. People use this information to quickly help them determine if your website contains what they're looking for.

Now What?

Now it's time to select your keywords, meta description, and meta title. Even if you're unfamiliar with website coding, adding these to your website is a fairly simple process.

When writing your meta description and meta title, you want to have your most important keywords in there. For example, If you are selling "blue widgets," then your meta title may be "Largest Blue Widget Inventory Online." And your meta description may be "Looking for the Largest Blue Widget Inventory Online? We have more than 1 Million Blue Widgets for you to choose from."

Here's what the keywords, meta title, and meta description look like on our website.

Be sure that your keywords, meta title, and meta description match the keyword (or keyword phrase) that your prospective visitors would type into their search engine of choice.

More FREE SEO Tools

Google provides some really useful tools. And lucky for us, they're free.

Below are a few of my favorites. They'll be very useful to you in starting the optimization of your website for search engines.

SO YOU HAVE A WEBSITE NOW WHAT 55

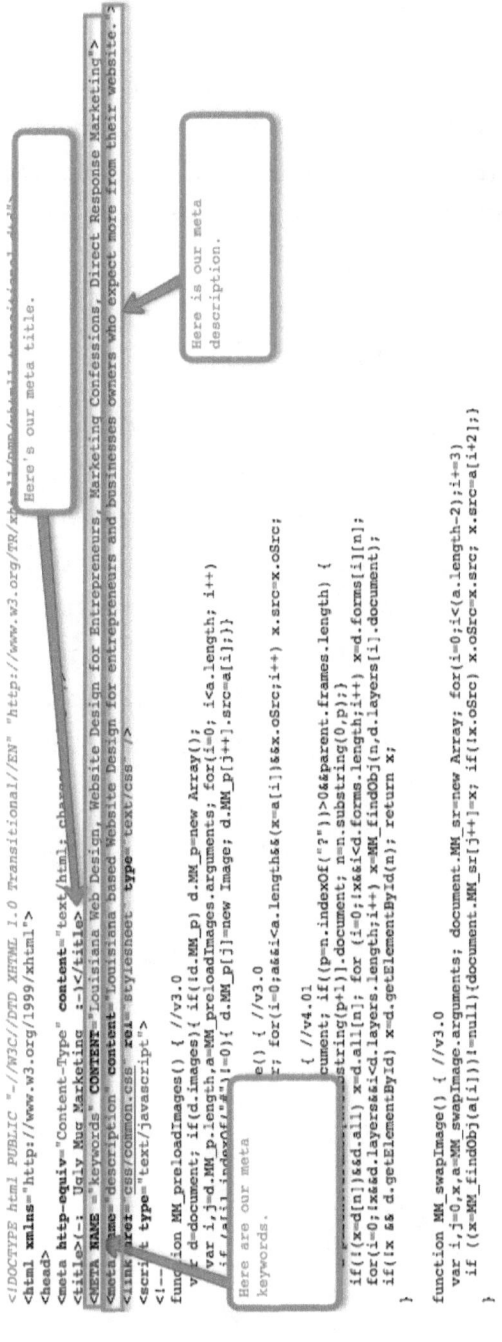

Related Search

By entering your keyword and typing "related search," Google will reveal all other search terms people use when searching for your keyword. You can see above, in this case, Google provided us with an additional fifteen related search terms that we could possibly use as keywords.

Wonder Wheel Magic

The Google Wonder Wheel is probably one of my favorite SEO tools. It gives a quick visual of all the related keywords.

You can see that our "primary" keyword is in the middle, and all of the "related" keywords are around the wheel. Now you can see the other words people may be using to search for what you provide. Now for the magic: if you click any of the related keywords around the wheel, you'll discover all the keywords that are related to that particular keyword.

SO YOU HAVE A WEBSITE NOW WHAT 57

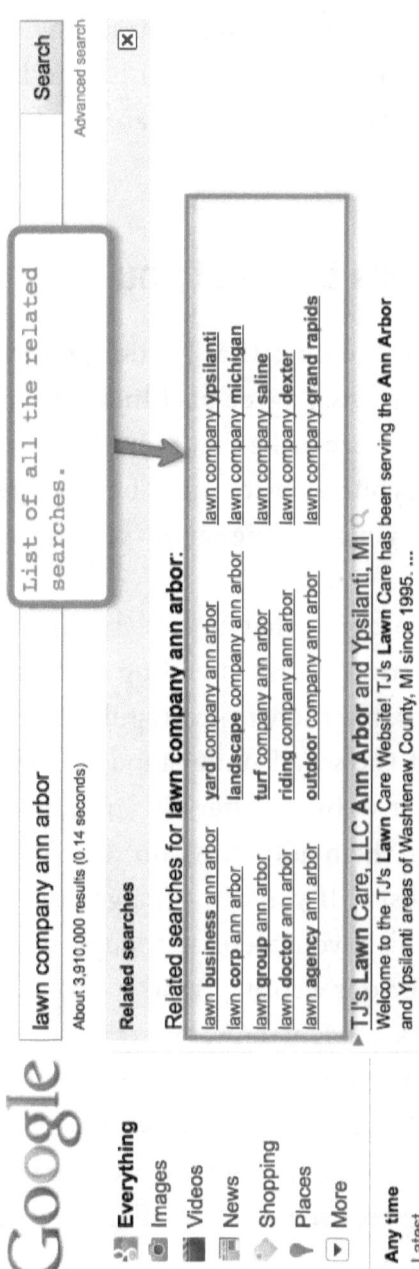

Before you spend the next three hours playing with the Wonder Wheel, it's best to keep your mission in mind. Find keywords that your prospects may use when searching for your product or service online.

Pointing Their ~~Fingers~~ Links at You

All SEO gurus (at least all the ones that I follow, which are some of the best in the business) agree backlinks are important. As a general rule, the more links that point to your website, the more important your website must be. As a result, your website should be displayed higher in search engine results.

These same gurus also agree that not all backlinks are created equal. Backlinks from websites ending with .edu or .gov tend to be more favorable than from "regular" websites. Here's why—well, at least the way I understand it: Anybody can get a link from another website. After all, you can simply call your friends and have them add a link on their websites pointing back to your website. If you can get a governmental agency or a university to link to your website, though, you must have some valuable info on your website, right?

Maybe, maybe not. As of right now, though, the search engines believe your site must be providing some great info.

You may be thinking, "Geez! How in the world can I get a .edu or .gov website to link to mine?" Don't worry about it. At this point, it's not worth your time or effort. For now, simply worry about getting backlinks.

SO YOU HAVE A WEBSITE NOW WHAT

WARNING: The Google Wonder Wheel may be addictive.

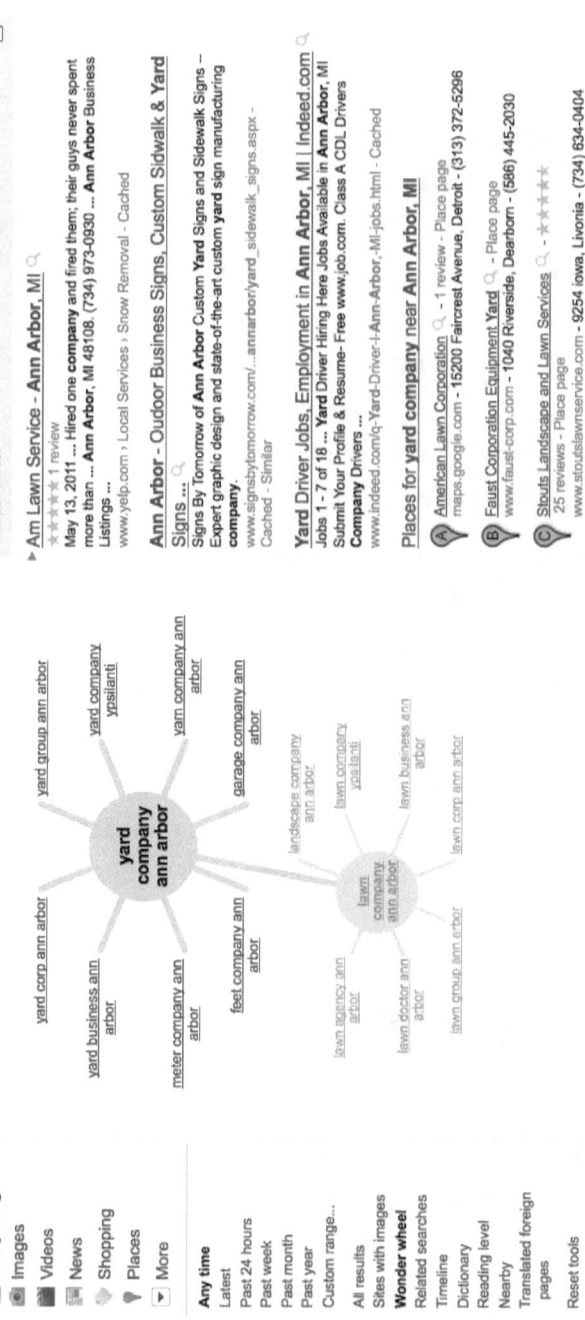

Anchors Away

Before you start working on getting backlinks pointing to your website, learn a little secret of getting the right kind of links.

Let's assume that your website address is www.uglymugmarketing.com. When you start placing links to your website, here's *what you definitely **don't** want to do*.

You can check out my website at <u>www.uglymugmarketing.com</u>.

Here's what you want to do:
Need help with <u>small business marketing</u>?

You want to make your keyword the anchor text for your backlinks. In this example, my keyword phrase would be "small business marketing," and people would be able to click the underlined portion. This approach tells search engines that the content on the page to which the anchor text is linking must be about small business marketing.

Now let's talk about why and how the domain name you choose effects what search engines think about the value of your website.

A Name with Meaning

Not all domain names are created equal. Some companies have paid millions just for their domain name. Why would someone be willing to pay so much for a domain name? The companies that pay this much aren't crazy; they understand that having the right domain name is a critical factor in online success.

Here are a few things to consider before selecting a domain name:

- **Domain age**—How long has the domain name been registered? (How long has there been a website at that particular domain name?) The longer it has been registered, the better. Search engines believe that the longer a domain name has been registered the more important it must be.

- **Keyword match**—Does the domain name match the keyword or keyword phrase people are using in their search? (For example, if your prospects were searching for "blue widgets," then it would be ideal to own the domain www.bluewidgets.com).

- **Audio test**—Quickly say the domain name you're considering to some of your friends and watch their reaction. If they ask you to repeat it, then you may need to keep looking.

- **Spelling test**—Is the domain name you're considering easy to spell? Could it be spelled several different ways? You'll ideally want a name that is simple to spell. Avoid words that could be spelled a variety of ways. (For example, *no* and *know*.)

- **.com, .net, .info**—Not all domain extensions are created equal. (A domain extension is what appears at the end of your domain name. For example, .com, .net, .info) When most people hear a domain name, they usually automatically hear and **think .com**. If at all possible, try to purchase the .com extension of your domain name.

<h1>Tags</h1>

Strategically using tags will help boost the effectiveness of your search engine optimization efforts. Tags are used for headings and headlines on websites (typically the sections with the boldest and largest font). There are six types of tags: <h1> to <h6> tags. The <h1> tag defines the most important heading and the <h6> tag defines the least important heading.

As search engine spiders scan a website's code, they take into consideration the words that appear between these tags. Search engine spiders assume that the words inside the tags must be what that particular web page is about. Let's look at an example together:

<h1>The World's Largest Selection of Blue Widgets</h1>

If the phrase above appeared on a website, it would appear as a big, bold font. (Obviously, the <h1> and </h1> tags would be displayed since they are part of the html code.)

The search engine spiders notice the words "The World's Largest Selection of Blue Widgets," and assume that the web page must be about the world's largest selection of blue widgets. If the page wasn't about that, why would the website owner have placed that phrase in <h1> tags (that is, large, bold font).

If you're using WordPress, you can easily assign tags to sentences from inside the post or page editor. Even if you're not using WordPress, your web designer or developer can easily add or change the text that appears inside tags.

For the best SEO results, you'll want the phrases inside your tags to match the keywords or keyword phrases that your ideal site visitors would type into a search engine.

That's All Folks

That concludes our section on search engine optimization. At this point, you'll typically fall into one of two categories: you'll either be completely overwhelmed, or you'll still be looking and hoping for a "magic bullet." My advice to both groups is the same: pick one thing and work on it today.

For those overwhelmed, don't be. SEO isn't about overnight success. Nothing in life is. Pick one of the above ideas, and apply it to your website. Keep learning and experimenting with your website, and you'll begin seeing results.

For those still looking for the magic bullet, it's not here. Sorry! There are plenty of "get rich quick through the Internet" books, courses and seminars available. This isn't one of them. My advice is that you give up your search for the magic bullet; instead, select one of the areas above and begin implementing it in your business.

Key point: In SEO, the tortoise beats the hare!

But with pay per click, the hare often beats the tortoise. Let's discuss a few pay-per-click techniques.

Pay-Per-Click Advertising

Pay per click (**PPC**) is a form of Internet advertising used to direct traffic to a website. In this form, the advertiser pays the search engine company (or another website owner) when the ad is clicked. With search engines, advertisers typically bid on keywords and keyword phrases relevant to their target market. Website owners typically charge a fixed price per click rather than using a bidding system.

By utilizing PPC advertising, you can start sending traffic to your website in a matter of hours, not days. In this section, we will discuss how you can set up a Google Adwords campaign along with some of the common mistakes people make when setting up their PPC campaigns.

The first step is setting up your Adwords account. You can do this by visiting: https://adwords.google.com

Follow the instructions, and you should have your account set up in about fifteen minutes. Once your account is set up, Google will try to bring you step by step through the process of creating your first ad campaign—***but*** *don't follow their advice* and use defaults (I'm referring to their advice once your account is set up).

Remember, Google makes money based on the number of times people click on your ad, so naturally they want you to spend as much as possible. During this section, we'll discuss how to maximize the effectiveness of your Adwords campaigns while also keeping your budget as low as possible.

Creating a Campaign

Think for a minute about your business, and look back over the keywords research you did earlier. You're going to want to group your keywords into categories. For example, if you have a lawn and landscape company, you may use the following categories of keywords and phrases: lawn care, landscaping, irrigation, and lawn fertilization.

Now, here are a few examples of keywords that may be under each of those categories:

> **Lawn care**—lawn maintenance, lawn mowing, lawn care company, etc.
>
> **Landscaping**—landscape maintenance, landscape installation, landscaper, etc.
>
> **Irrigation**—irrigation installation, irrigation maintenance, irrigation repair, etc.
>
> **Lawn fertilization**—lawn fertilizer, lawn fertilizer application, etc.

When setting up your first campaign, select one category. (You'll eventually create a separate campaign for each category of keywords.)

Step 1

For your first campaign, select the keyword category of your business that represents the section of your business you are most interested in growing. For our example, I'll select the landscaping category.

Also make a few manual selections regarding where Google will display your ads. Remember, Google makes money every time someone clicks your ad(s)—regardless of their intent. Your goal is only to have your ad clicked by people who are serious about purchasing your products or services.

Take a look at the following screen shot for how you should initially set up your campaign:

Initially, you will only want your ads displayed in Google search. Once you start running your campaign, you'll be able to measure and monitor the effects of having your ad displayed with other "Search partners" and the "Display Network."

Next, you can select what type of devices you want your ads to display on. Think about your target audience. Would they likely purchase your products or services from their smartphone or tablet device? If so, then you'll want to have your ads displayed when people search from these devices.

Under "Bidding Options," select "Advanced Options." This will give you more control over how you bid on keywords and the rate that your ads will be displayed.

SO YOU HAVE A WEBSITE NOW WHAT 69

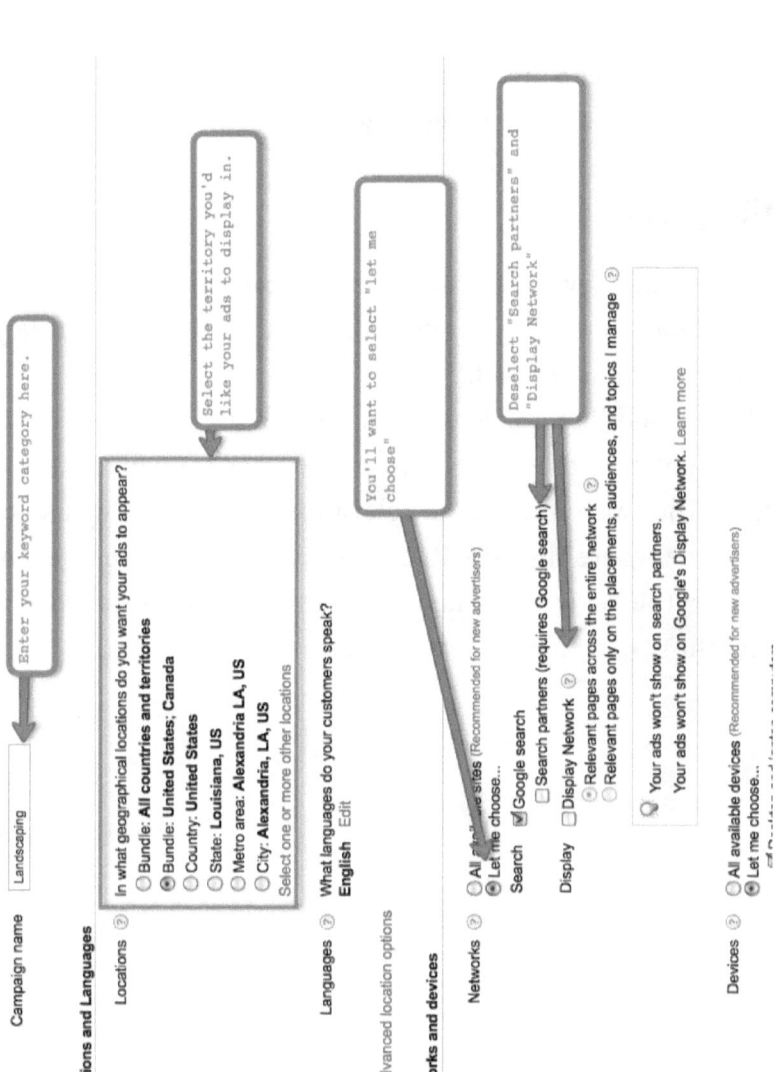

For the "Delivery Method," choose "Accelerated." I realize that it seems like a good idea to have Google display your ads evenly over time, but it isn't. You want to have complete and total control over when and how your ads are displayed.

To move to the next step in setting up your campaign, enter your "Budget" (this is your daily budget). For now, you may want to just enter $1.00.

Now it's time to put together your first campaign.

Writing Ads

Getting good at writing words that sell can take practice. The trick is to select one of your keywords and use that specific keyword throughout your ad.

When bidding on keywords (which we'll get to later), Google not only takes into account the amount you're willing to pay. They also have an ad relevance algorithm they use to determine where the ad will be displayed. The more relevant the ad to the keyword or keyword phrase being searched, the better the display position of the ad.

SO YOU HAVE A WEBSITE NOW WHAT 71

Devices ⓘ ○ All available devices (Recommended for new advertisers)
          ● Let me choose...
              ☑ Desktop and laptop computers
              ☑ Mobile devices with full browsers
              ☑ Tablets with full browsers
              ⊞ Advanced mobile and tablet options

> In the past we use to recommend that people only allow ads to display on desktops, but with the ever increasing use of internet on tablets and phones you may want to consider having your ads display on all these devices.

Bidding and budget

Bidding option ⓘ   Basic options | Advanced options
                   ● Focus on **clicks** - use maximum CPC bids
                   ● Manual bidding for clicks
                       ○ You'll set your maximum CPC bids in the next step.
                   ○ Automatic bidding to try to maximize clicks for your target budget
                   Enhanced CPC ⓘ
                   ☐ Use my conversion tracking data and bids to optimize for conversions
                       Unavailable because conversion tracking isn't set up. Setup conversion tracking.
                   ○ Focus on **conversions** (Conversion Optimizer) - use CPA bids
                       Unavailable because conversion tracking isn't set up. Setup conversion tracking.
                   ○ Focus on **impressions** - use maximum CPM bids
                       Unavailable because this campaign is running on Google Search or the Search Network.

> Select "Advanced Options"

> Select "Manual bidding for clicks"

Budget ⓘ $ [   ] per day (Format: 25.00)
           Actual daily spend may vary. ⓘ

☐ Delivery method (advanced)

Delivery method ⓘ   ○ Standard: Show ads evenly over time
                    ● Accelerated: Show ads as quickly as possible
                    ⓘ You may miss traffic later in the day if you choose accelerated delivery. Learn more

> Select "Accelerated" you don't want to give Google control over when your ads display.

> Standard delivery is recommended for most advertisers. Learn more

Adding Keywords

Now it's time to add the keywords your ideal prospects are searching to your Adwords campaign. By adding keywords, you are telling Google on which search terms and phrases you want to bid. This is when the keyword research you did previously becomes invaluable.

Technically, Google will allow you to add as many keywords as your fingers would like to type. *But don't.* Sure, it's amazing to think that you can get visitors to your website from dozens and dozens of different keywords. Google would love for you do just that; after all, they make money each time someone clicks on your ad.

Initially, you'll want to limit the number of keywords you enter to about a dozen (keywords or keyword phrases), at least until you get familiar with running your Adwords campaign.

> **Key point:** Add only keywords that closely match your ad "Headline" (see below). This improves your ad relevance, which Google loves and reportedly rewards.

SO YOU HAVE A WEBSITE NOW WHAT

Create ad and keywords

Create an ad

◉ Text ad   ○ Image ad   ○ Display ad builder   ○ WAP mobile ad

Now it's time to write your first ad! To appeal to customers searching for your product or service, highlight what sets you apart from the competition, and use clear, specific text. Help me write a great text ad.

Headline	Landscape Installation
Description line 1	Landscape Installation that makes
Description line 2	neighbors jealous guaranteed!
Display URL ⓘ	UglyMugLawnCare.com/Landscape
Destination URL ⓘ	https:// ▾ nCare.com/Landscape-Installation

You can see what I've done is use one of keywords as the Headline and then repeated the phrase again in my Description and in my URL

Ad preview: The following ad previews may be formatted slightly differently from what is shown to users. Learn more

Side ad

> Landscape Installation
> Landscape Installation that makes neighbors jealous guaranteed!
> UglyMugLawnCare.com/Landscape

Top ad

Landscape Installation
Landscape Installation that makes neighbors jealous guaranteed!
UglyMugLawnCare.com/Landscape

Ad extensions expand your ad with additional information like a business address or product images.
Take a tour.

Keywords

You can see from the image above I've entered keywords that match the headline from my ad.

You're Sooo Negative

When it comes to your Adwords account, it pays to be negative. When you enter a keyword like "landscape installation" into your Adwords account, Google automatically assumes that you want your ad to display every time someone does a search containing any combination of words or phrases with that keyword term.

For example, when you enter "landscape installation," Google assumes you'd like your ad to appear when someone searches for "discount landscape installation," or "landscape installation that is cheap."

Displaying your ad when people search for these terms may be good if you're a discount landscape contractor. However, if you provide premium landscape installation, why would you want to waste your money on people looking for cheap or discount landscape installation?

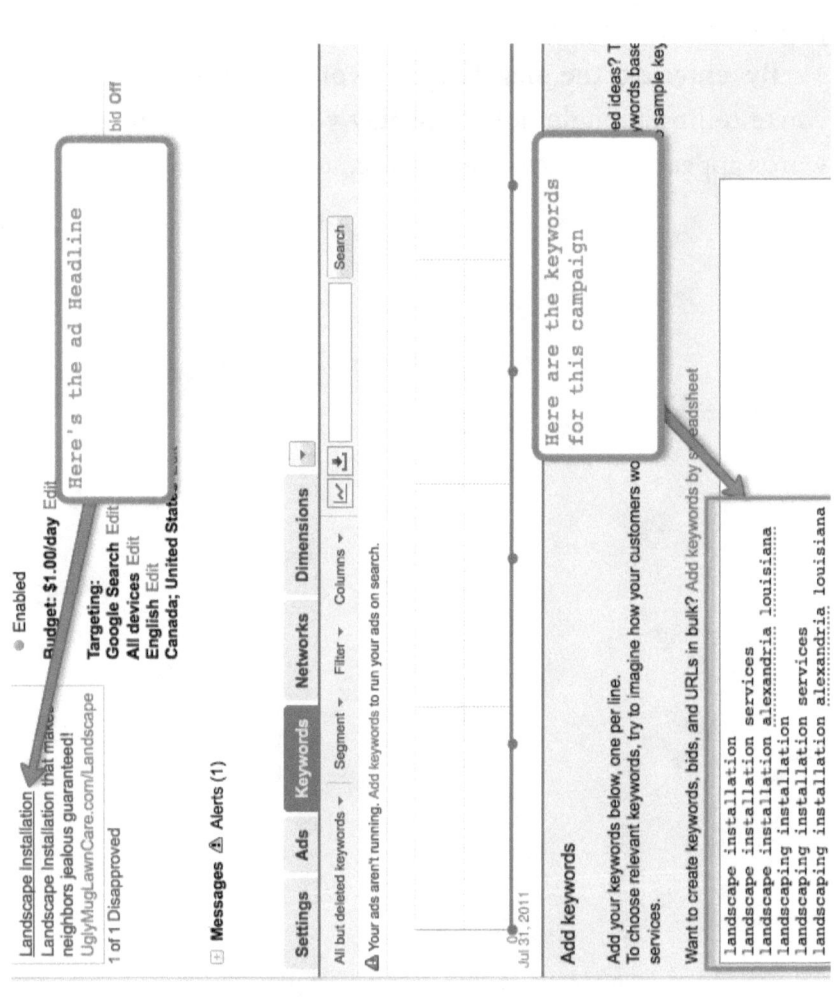

You wouldn't, right? So this is when it pays to be negative.

Google gives you the ability to keep your ad from displaying when certain keywords are being searched. Take a look at the image below, and you'll see how to tell Google when not to display your ad.

By entering the negative keywords *discount* and *cheap*, you're telling Google not to display your ads any time those words appear in the keyword phrase.

SO YOU HAVE A WEBSITE NOW WHAT

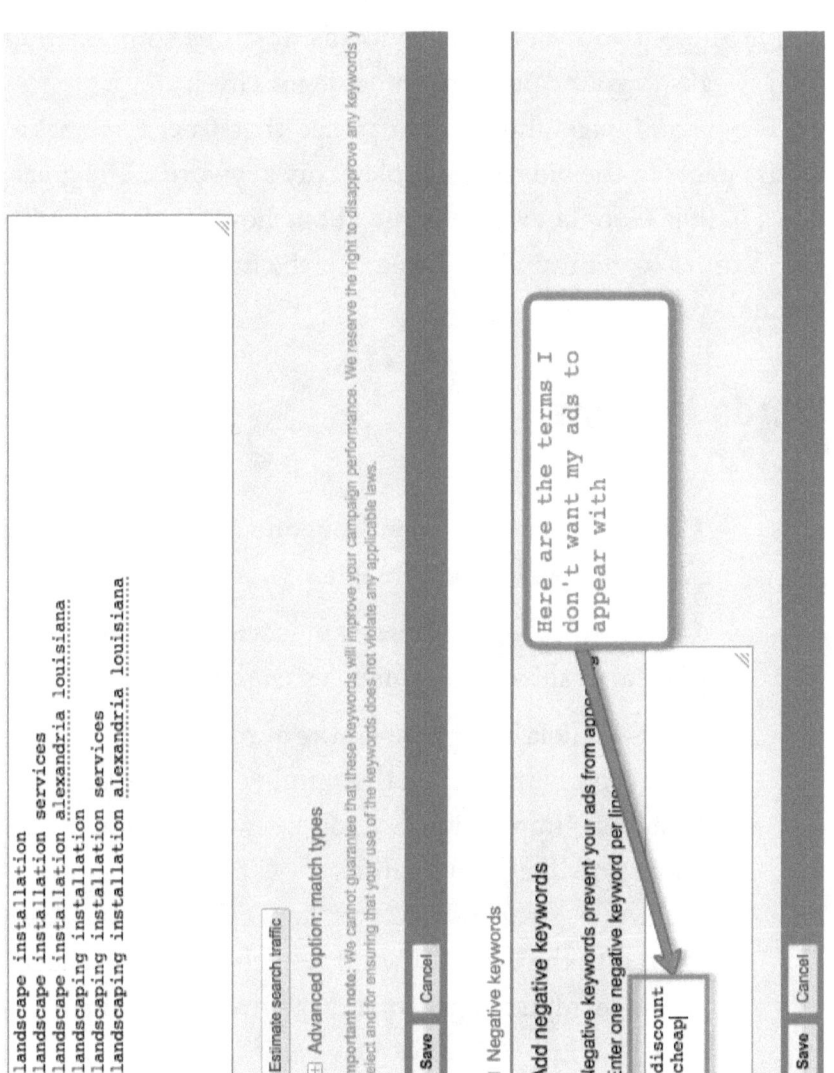

Last-Minute Adjustments

Now you've written a great ad. You've entered your keywords. You've entered your negative keywords. It's time to make the final tweaks to your campaign before it goes live.

From the image above, you can see that I need to make adjustments to the bids on a couple of my keywords. The great news is that Google even tells me about how much I should bid in order to get my ad to display on the first page of search results.

Words to Know

Clicks—A click is when someone clicks on your ad. (This is when you pay Google.)

Impressions—An impression is when your ad is displayed, or shown, in someone's search results.

CTR—Clickthrough rate is the number of clicks your ad receives, divided by the number of times your ad is shown (impressions). Each keyword in your campaign will likely have a different CTR. Your keyword CTR is a great indicator of how relevant your keyword is to the user. A low CTR likely means you need to make adjustments to your keywords and/or your ad.

☐	Keyword	Status ②	Max. CPC	Clicks ②	Impr.	CTR ②	Avg. CPC ②	Cost	Avg. Pos.
☐ ●	landscape installation	☐ Below first page bid First page bid estimate: $0.65	$0.50 ☒						
☐ ●	landscaping installation	☐ Below first page bid First page bid estimate: $1.00	$0.50 ☒						
☐ ●	landscape installation services	☐ Eligible	$0.50 ☒	0	0	0.00%	$0.00	$0.00	0
☐ ●	landscaping installation services	☐ Eligible	$0.50 ☒	0	0	0.00%	$0.00	$0.00	0
☐ ●	landscaping installation alexandria louisiana	☐ Low search volume ②	$0.50 ☒	0	0	0.00%	$0.00	$0.00	0
☐ ●	landscape installation alexandria louisiana	☐ Low search volume ②	$0.50 ☒	0	0	0.00%	$0.00	$0.00	0
	Total - Search ②			0	0	0.00%	$0.00	$0.00	
	Total - Display Network ②			0	0	0.00%	$0.00	$0.00	
	Total - all keywords			0	0	0.00%	$0.00	$0.00	

Notice Google is warning us that our bid for these may be too low.

They are also warning that the search volume for these keyword phrases is low.

Show rows: 50 ▼ 1 - 6 of 6

⊟ Negative keywords

+ Add | Edit | Delete | Download

☐ Negative keyword

☐ discount

Average CPC—This is simply the average amount you pay each time someone clicks on your ad. Totaling the cost of all your clicks and then dividing it by the number of clicks determines your average CPC.

Average position—Average position is simply in what position your ad is displayed. Typically (but not always), the higher the position the better CTR you'll receive.

Spread the Wealth

Once you're familiar with Google Adwords, it's time to start experimenting with Bing and Yahoo PPC. Although neither of these has as much search volume each month as Google, they also don't have as many advertisers competing for the same keywords. We often receive higher clickthrough rates on Yahoo and Bing than on Google. Keeping that in mind, it's still best to test your skills using Google first.

Social Media

Harnessing the Power of Facebook

It took radio thirty-eight years to reach fifty million users. It took TV thirteen years, the Internet four years, and iPod just three years. But Facebook added one hundred million users in just nine months. Wow! What's the deal? How is Facebook growing so quickly?

Facebook is built on the idea that people like to be connected and share experiences with acquaintances, friends, and loved ones. So it capitalizes on those connections.

- The fastest growing segment of Facebook is women ages fifty-five to sixty-five.
- If Facebook were a country, it would have the third-largest population behind only China and India.
- One out of every twelve people in the world has a Facebook account.

- One out of every four people in America has a Facebook account.
- Facebook is currently growing at a rate of about seven hundred thousand people a day.
- Facebook hosts over fifteen billion photos on its site, and people upload one hundred million more every day.

What happens every sixty seconds on Facebook?

- 510,404 comments
- 382,861 posts liked
- 231,605 messages sent
- 135,849 photos added
- 98,604 friendships approved
- 82,557 status updates
- 79,364 Wall posts
- 74,204 event invites received
- 72,816 pages liked
- 66,168 photos tagged

Still not convinced that Facebook can be a valuable marketing tool for your business? Don't worry, neither am I.

Sure, *lots* of people are using Facebook these days, but does that mean that it can help you grow your business? After not using Facebook for over a year, I'll be the first to admit that Facebook won't benefit every business. But my reason may not be what you think it is: The truth is…

Facebook is only a tool.

And like any other tool, it must be used if it's going to work for you. The more efficient you become at using the tool, the more value the tool will bring to your business.

This is a problem for most business owners. They don't have the time and discipline to learn how to use Facebook effectively to grow their businesses.

This means, as a business owner, you are left with three choices:

1. Learn how to utilize the tool and reap the benefits.
2. Utilize the tool poorly and don't reap the benefits.
3. Completely ignore the tool and expect zero benefits.

I challenge you to take the first choice. Do your best to embrace the challenge, roll up your sleeves, and start learning. You agree? Okay, great! Let's get started by talking about how to advertise effectively on Facebook.

The Secret to Effective Facebook Ads

Facebook ads work in much the same manner as Google Adwords. You create an ad, set a few variables indicating whom you would like to reach, and set your budget. The process actually takes less time than setting up an Adwords campaign, and it can yield better results than Adwords when it is done correctly.

The Facebook Demographic Advantage

Facebook has a strong advantage over Google, Bing, and Yahoo: you are able to choose who will see your ads based on very specific demographic criteria and user likes and interest. Facebook is able to offer ads in this manner because you must be a registered to use Facebook; and when you register as a user, you have to provide them with this information.

Using these criteria gives you a more direct path to your ideal prospects. For example, if you sell a small business marketing program, you can choose to advertise to those that have the following interests: marketing, business, business growth, advertising, and promotion. I'm sure you agree that displaying your ad to people interested in these topics would be very beneficial. Let's take a look at exactly how you can set up and target your Facebook campaign.

Where Should Your Ad Point?

Facebook would prefer that your Facebook ads point people to your Facebook page. After all, this would keep the person on Facebook and not send them outside to your website. However, you can choose an external URL (meaning a site outside of Facebook) to send your prospects to. You'll simply need to click the External URL option on the Destination drop-down list, and simply type in your URL.

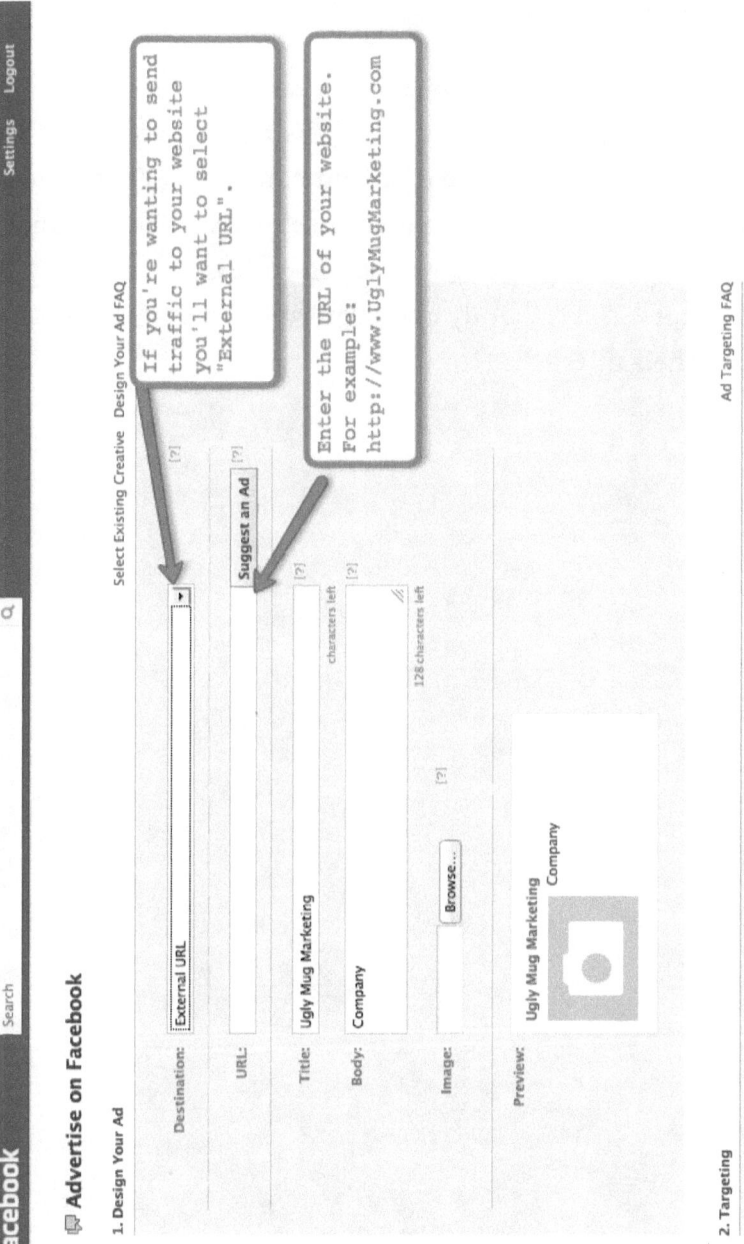

Writing Your Facebook Ad

Once you've entered the URL where you'd like to send people, it's time to write your ad. The title for your ad is vitally important to the success of your campaign. Your headline needs to capture attention and raise interest. Unfortunately, all of those things need to happen in less than twenty-five characters. Your ad body gives you 135 characters to continue pique their interest.

SO YOU HAVE A WEBSITE NOW WHAT

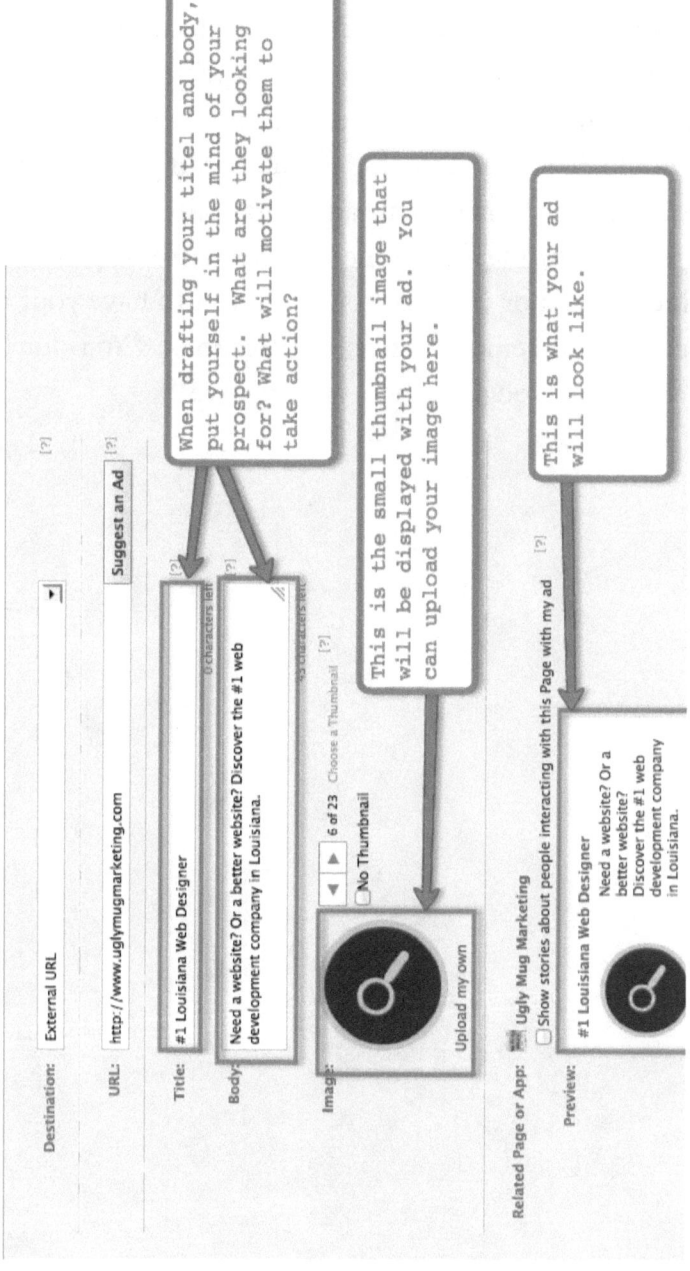

Location and Demographics

Next you'll have the ability to choose the location(s) you'd like to target. Your ads will appear only in the regions you select. Do you know the age and sex of your typical customer? If not, you should do some surveying to find out. If you already know, you can choose to have your ad appear only for the age range and sex of your ideal customer. For example, if you're selling products to senior citizens, you can select to have your ad displayed only to senior citizens on Facebook. (You don't have this ability on Google, Yahoo, or Bing—yet!)

SO YOU HAVE A WEBSITE NOW WHAT 89

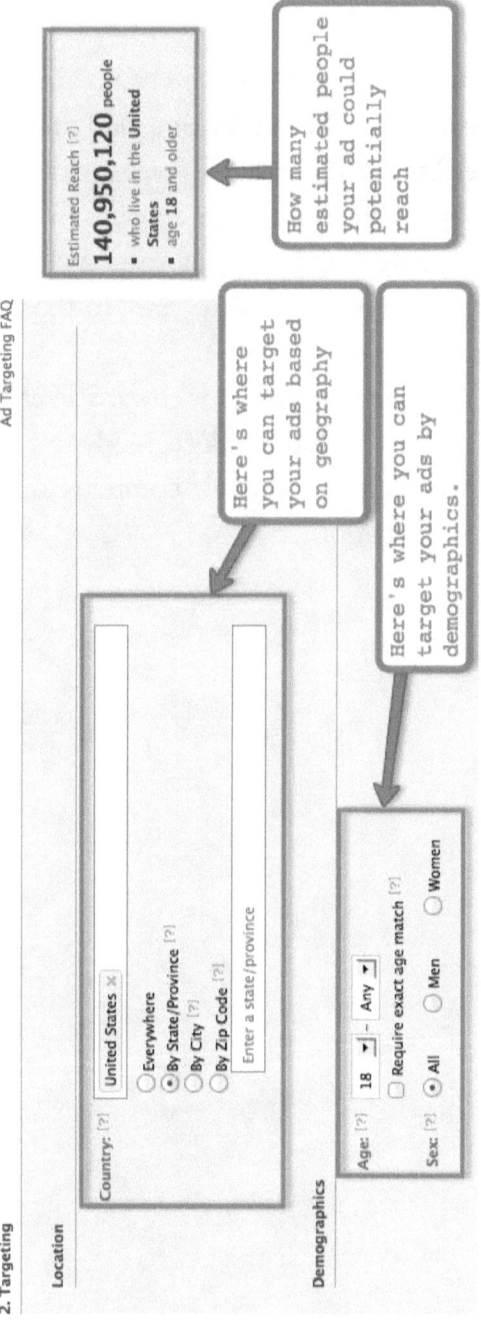

Education and Work

Again, the Education and Work data can really help you focus the reach of your ads. The Workplace field gives you unbelievable focus. Let's say that you have a website development company, and you're trying to sell your services to a large company in your area. By entering the company name in the Workplace field, you can have your ad appear only to those who work at that particular company.

If you choose to focus your ads toward a specific company, write your ads in a way that speaks directly to them. You don't want to focus your ads at a specific company and have it come off as generic or just another ad.

SO YOU HAVE A WEBSITE NOW WHAT   91

Relationship: [?] ☑ All   ☐ Single   ☐ Engaged
                              ☐ In a relationship   ☐ Married

Languages: [?] Enter language

Education & Work

Education: [?] ● All   ○ College Grad
                          ○ In College
                          ○ In High School

Workplaces: [?] Enter a company, organization or other workplace

Estimated Reach [?]
55,560 people
- who live in the **United States**
- who live in **Louisiana**
- age **18** and older
- who like **#Business, #Marketing #Social**

> Let's say you want to target a very specific company. If they have a Facebook page, you can enter type the company name here and your ad will then only appear to those who have "liked" their Facebook page.

⊟ Hide Advanced Targeting Options

Ad Campaigns and Pricing FAQ

3. Campaigns, Pricing and Scheduling

Campaign & Budget

Campaign Name: Win an iPod

Budget (USD): $3.00 daily budget ▼

Create a new campaign [?]

Schedule

Campaign Schedule: 09/27/2011 10:30am – Ongoing

Budget, Bidding, and Schedule

Don't worry; you are almost finished setting up your campaign. In the last few fields, you'll enter your budget, set your campaign schedule, and set your ad bid amount. When setting your budget, you'll have the option to set it based on a daily budget or on a campaign lifetime budget. By setting a lifetime budget, you're campaign will run until it reaches the budget you set. The same is true of setting a daily budget. The only difference is that using a daily budget removes your ad each day once you reach your budget.

Under the Schedule section, you have the ability to set a specific date range and the times you'd like your ad to run. With a little research, you can find out exactly when your target audience is most likely to be on Facebook. With this valuable knowledge, you can choose to run your ads during this time.

In the final section, you'll get to choose between paying for impressions and paying for clicks. It's usually better to start with paying per click. This ensures that you're paying only for the traffic that actually ends up on your website. Having a lot of impressions doesn't mean much, because it's difficult to make money or build a following on people who have only had the chance to see your ad.

Like Google, Yahoo, and Bing, Facebook provides you with a recommended bid range. As much as I hate to admit it, you're usually going to be better off setting your bid within the range that Facebook recommends. However, feel free to experiment and see what bid yields the highest CTR (clickthrough rate). You can do this by simply duplicating the exact same ad and setting a different bid amount on the second one.

SO YOU HAVE A WEBSITE NOW WHAT 93

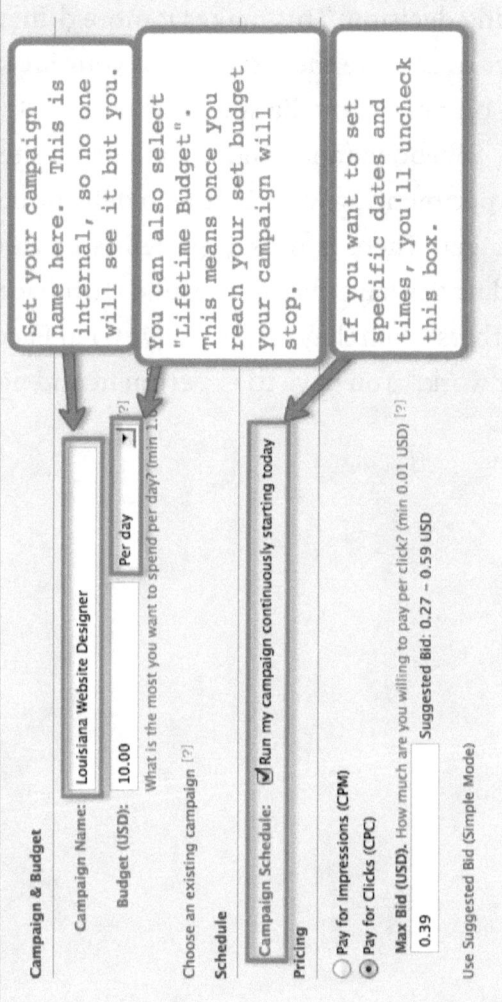

The Disadvantage of Social Media

Advertising on Facebook has a definite disadvantage compared to other search engines. Think for a minute about your own use of Facebook or any other social media. When you're on Facebook, more than likely you aren't looking to purchase a product or service. You're on there to relax and be entertained, not to make a purchasing decision. This makes it more difficult for you as an advertiser to capture the attention of your ideal prospects while they're on a social media site.

That being said, Facebook (and other social media sites) are definitely worth experimenting with, if only to determine what type of results you get. There is no set guideline or rule that tells you which industries have the best results with Facebook. So don't listen to others when they say, "Oh, I've tried Facebook ads, and they don't work." You have to experiment and figure it out for yourself.

Thirteen Questions

Having a website built, or an existing website redesigned, can (*and should*) be a very enjoyable process, but you need to be prepared. The key to a smooth process is being clearly informed about exactly what you're getting, and exactly what your total investment will be.

The following questions will help ensure you don't get burned and help make sure that you're thrilled at the end of your website project:

1. What is your design process?
    a. *It's important they have a clearly defined process they follow to insure your success and happiness. We utilize the 3 C's of good design...but we do them in reverse order. This is crucial to making your website work for you.*
2. Can you give me a breakdown of the total cost of ownership I will incur for the website? (What are the costs to keep the site updated, for hosting, security updates, etc.?)

a. *Be sure you get a detailed proposal along with a Service Agreement or Contract prior to beginning the project.*

3. How will you keep my site secure? (Sony, Bank of America, Amazon.com and other Fortune 500 have all had their websites hacked.)

    a. *Sure, we take lots of steps to help insure your website is safe, but if hackers can get into Fortune 500 companies' websites, there's a chance they could hack yours. So it's important to be sure your website source files are backed up on a regular basis.*

4. What happens when I want to make a change on the website? (Do I have to pay? Can I do it myself? Is it a flat fee or hourly rate if I have to have you make the changes?)

    a. *With the abundance and affordability of CMS (Content Management Systems), it really makes sense to have your website built using CMS. These systems will give you the ability to make changes to your website without any coding knowledge.*

5. Can you provide references from 5 companies for whom you have built websites?

    a. *Look for specific comments regarding the design and building processes. Be sure the references have positive things to say about them.*

6. How many websites have you developed utilizing CMS (Content Management Systems)?

    a. *Ideally you want to work with a designer who has designed/built at least 6 websites utilizing their chosen*

CMS. *You don't want them experimenting and learning on your dime, do you?*

7. Can you give me a list of at least 15 websites you have built?

    a. *Be sure they have a strong portfolio. If they don't...ask why.*

8. Who will own the Intellectual Property Rights to my website?

    a. *If you're paying someone to design and build your website, don't you want to own it? It's shocking how many designers try to maintain ownership of the design and source files. Be sure they agree to give you all the Photoshop files, as well as the code source files.*

9. Is the website portable (i.e. can I move it off of your system)? Who can host the website?

    a. *You'll want to be sure you can host your website on any server, with any major hosting company. This will help insure that your designer/coder doesn't use some "extinct" programming language.*

10. Is the website scalable (can we add additional pages or features in the future)?

    a. *As your business grows so should your website. Be sure that your designer builds a site that will allow for expansion without having to be completely redesigned.*

11. How long will it take to design, code, and implement my website?

    a. *You'll want to find a happy middle ground here. If they* are promising too quick of a turnaround, chances are they will be using a template for your website. If the time frame is too long, it's usually a good indication they don't have good processes in place.

12. Will a template be utilized to design my website?
    a. *Unfortunately some designers charge for custom design, and then utilize a website template. You can test this by asking if there will be any limitations with regards to your design.*

13. Will you be able to design my site to look exactly how I want it to look?
    a. *Designing your website to your taste is good, but wouldn't it be better to design according your prospects and clients' tastes?*

If you take the time to ask each of these questions, you'll have a very good understanding of exactly what to expect and when to expect it while working with your designer.

You and I Are the Same

We are very similar. You see, I didn't grow up around computers. I didn't major in information technology or programming. Although I grew up in a middle-class family, we didn't have a computer in our house until I had already started college. Computers and everything about them were completely foreign to me. I knew nothing about websites and how they work.

I didn't start learning and experimenting with websites until I had my first website. And when I started, everything seemed like a mystery to me. I had no clue what I was looking at or what I was doing. But I kept learning, kept experimenting, kept making mistakes, and, most importantly, I keep trying. And if you're going to succeed, you have to be willing to do the same.

The ~~End~~ Beginning Is Near

You're only a few paragraphs away from finishing this book, and your head is probably full of ideas, questions, and even fears.

With that in mind, I have a serious question to ask: Will this be the end or just the beginning for you?

For a number of people, this would be the end. They would tell themselves that they simply don't have the time, talent, and resources necessary to take their website to the next level.

I'm reminded of a quote: "Whether you think you can or can't, you're right!"

You're not in this category; otherwise you wouldn't still be reading this book. You are someone who takes action. You expect more from your website, and you're willing to do whatever is necessary to get more from it.

I've tried to lay out this book in a logical sequence that anyone can follow. When followed, this plan will yield results that you can see. Resist the temptation to feel overwhelmed.

Remember: A journey of a thousand miles begins with one step.

The most important thing is to take action. You can do it. I know you can!

THANKS

Thanks to our clients who have endured our crazy ideas and provided more inspiration and encouragement than they realize. To Jim Clinton and Gary Perkins, thanks for giving me a chance. To Larry Freeborg, thanks for challenging me to push the edges of my comfort zone. To Dirk Margheim, thanks for encouraging me to keep pushing forward. Seth Godin and Bassam Tarazi, thanks for your feedback and direction. A special thanks to Chris Farris for freeing me up to work on this project and for listening to all of my crazy ideas. Last but not least, thanks to *you* for taking the time to read something I've written. I hope you enjoy it.

ABOUT AUTHOR

Wayne Mullins is a passionate entrepreneur committed to being remarkable and getting extraordinary results for his clients. He regularly provides marketing insights to companies that are generating $1,000,000 to $100,000,000 in annual revenues. However, his passion is helping small business owners and entrepreneurs challenge their assumptions, creating value where they've never looked, and increasing their profits along the way. He has worked hands-on with clients in over 50 different business categories and from every corner of the globe.

Over the past 10 years, Wayne has started six companies, all with less than $1,000. His most recent creation, Ugly Mug Marketing, has helped clients around the world get more from their websites. Ugly Mug's work has won the praises of some of the top bloggers and influencers on the world wide web, such as... Neil Patel, Single Grain Digital Media, and MilitaryAvenue.com.

Over 100,000 people read his blog MarketingConfessions.com annually. Wayne's manifesto, *Confessions of a Dying Man*, has been downloaded over 5,000 times in the past three months.

Special Free Gift from the Author

The Most Incredible FREE ($497.00) Gift for You and Your Website

Yes! I want to take you up on The Most Incredible FREE ($497.00) Gift for Me and My Website

Here's what you'll get:

- The full 30-day course: Making an Online Money Machine – how to turn ordinary websites into cash-generating machines, which includes:
    - Why Most Websites Never Make Money
    - How to Get Traffic to Your Website in 2 Hours or Less
    - The 13 Questions You MUST Ask Before Hiring a Web Designer
    - Secrets to Discovering What Your Prospects Want

- Special Interview with international branding expert David Brier – How Ordinary Brands Become Extraordinary.

- A complimentary website review from the professionals at Wayne's company Ugly Mug Marketing.

To take advantage of this Incredible Free Gift – and discover how to outsmart your competitors – visit www.WebsiteNow-What.com/gift.

www.ingramcontent.com/pod-product-compliance
Lightning Source LLC
Chambersburg PA
CBHW030820180526
45163CB00003B/1360